PRUNING MADE EASY

PRUNING MADE EASY

The complete guide to perfect pruning, step-by-step

PETER McHOY

southwater

This edition is published by Southwater

Southwater is an imprint of Anness Publishing Ltd
Hermes House, 88–89 Blackfriars Road, London SE1 8HA
tel. 020 7401 2077; fax 020 7633 9499
www.southwaterbooks.com; info@anness.com

© Anness Publishing Ltd 1999, 2004

UK agent: The Manning Partnership Ltd, 6 The Old Dairy, Melcombe Road, Bath BA2 3LR;
tel. 01225 478444; fax 01225 478440; sales@manning-partnership.co.uk

UK distributor: Grantham Book Services Ltd, Isaac Newton Way, Alma Park Industrial Estate, Grantham, Lincs NG31 9SD;
tel. 01476 541080; fax 01476 541061; orders@gbs.tbs-ltd.co.uk

North American agent/distributor: National Book Network, 4501 Forbes Boulevard, Suite 200, Lanham, MD 20706;
tel. 301 459 3366; fax 301 429 5746; www.nbnbooks.com

Australian agent/distributor: Pan Macmillan Australia, Level 18, St Martins Tower, 31 Market St, Sydney, NSW 2000;
tel. 1300 135 113; fax 1300 135 103; customer.service@macmillan.com.au

New Zealand agent/distributor: David Bateman Ltd, 30 Tarndale Grove, Off Bush Road, Albany, Auckland;
tel. (09) 415 7664; fax (09) 415 8892

A CIP catalogue record for this book is available from the British Library.

Publisher: Joanna Lorenz
Project Editor: Clare Nicholson
Designer: Ian Sandom
Photographer: John Freeman
Illustrator: Vana Haggerty

Previously published as *Successful Pruning*

1 3 5 7 9 10 8 6 4 2

CONTENTS

INTRODUCTION

When it comes to pruning, even experienced and competent gardeners tend to hesitate and cut with trepidation. Less experienced gardeners usually pick up the secateurs (pruning shears) with more than a trace of apprehension, asking themselves a series of worried questions, "What if I prune out all the important bits and it won't flower or fruit? What if I spoil the shape? What if I kill the plant?"

Relax. The best approach to pruning is to enjoy it, and, if possible, to see it as a creative job, one where you can help to shape and mould plants to make them more pleasing.

It is most unlikely that you will kill a shrub by pruning it, even if you get it all wrong. The worst that is likely to happen is that you will lose the next flush of flowers, or that you will miss a season's fruit. Even then, the plant may perform better than ever the following year. And you will be sure to remember what to do next time!

Established plants are surprisingly resilient, and there are often many ways to prune the same shrub. Put these facts together and you should be reassured that if you get something a little wrong it probably won't be a disaster. It could even work out better than you expect.

A good example of this was made clear to me when I pruned a rose at a well-known garden for a gardening demonstration. It was winter, and although the label appeared to be missing, the staff were adamant that they knew exactly what type of rose the subject was. So I pruned it according to the method recommended for that type of rose. When much of the growth had been removed, however, a grubby label was discovered, identifying the rose as one that, according to the theory, should have been pruned in an entirely different way.

Guilt lay heavy – the summer display had probably been ruined. However, when I visited the garden during the summer, the bush was covered with a mound of flowers – it had actually flowered better than normal.

Rose pruning is a subject that has been treated with a degree of reverence, and earlier books gave very precise and detailed instructions. We then thought of pruning in a rough-and-ready way, without too much regard to counting buds, measuring stems, or cutting to buds pointing in a particular direction. And in what must have seemed like heresy to some traditionalists, an even cruder method was tried – shearing roses with a powered

hedge trimmer (shears). The two cruder methods of pruning were staggeringly successful, resulting in displays that tended to be better than the results of conventional pruning.

While these examples are reassuring, they are not given to encourage a slapdash approach to pruning. You will almost always get better results if you follow the tried and tested advice. Usually it will not matter much if you cut a few centimetres or inches too high or too low, or if occasionally you cut out some new wood rather than old. The chances are you will still have a good display, and certainly a better one than if you had neglected the plant completely.

CONFLICTING ADVICE
Do not be surprised if you read apparently conflicting advice in different books and in magazines, as there are often two or more ways in which a shrub or fruit tree can be pruned. In the case of fruit, for instance, a commercial grower will follow a method that gives the highest yield for a given area, while someone with just a few fruit trees in the garden may have a different priority. Many ornamentals can also be pruned in a variety of ways.

In this book things have been kept as simple as possible. For example, a suggested technique for a large range of shrubs is to cut out the oldest third of the shoots because the instruction is easy to follow and simple to execute. Although this method may sometimes result in fewer flowers, there will always be a good display, and the shrub should remain reasonably compact, which is an important consideration for a small garden.

One method is not necessarily "better" than another, but the simpler the technique the more likely it is to be carried out properly. Do not be over-concerned about debates among the experts.

BUILDING CONFIDENCE
The best way to learn how to prune is to do it, then to observe the results. Seeing how growth is affected by what you do is the best way to understand why pruning helps and how it works. And you can apply your knowledge to shrubs that may not be listed in this book.

Do not just prune for the sake of it, however. Many shrubs will grow for years without pruning, and this particularly applies to many evergreen foliage shrubs. Pruning these could spoil their shape. Be prepared to experiment, but also accept that it may be best to leave alone those shrubs that you are already happy with.

Opposite: *Formal hedges (those neatly clipped to a regular shape) need trimming if your garden is to look tidy. Using the right techniques will make your hedge look smarter, and enable the job to be done more quickly. This hedge has been clipped with a hedge trimmer (shears).*

Right: *Weeping standards should be pruned annually to ensure that they do not become too congested and that the head does not become top-heavy. They are pruned once the flowering display is over. In the spring, if the growth looks uneven, cut back the longest shoots to create a more balanced effect. This variety is* 'Excelsa'.

TECHNIQUES

Pruning Principles

There are probably many different shrubs in your garden, but the principles of pruning are relatively few, and easy to remember. If you grasp the fundamentals, you should be able to tackle your pruning with confidence – even if your plant looks nothing like the one in the picture.

CONTROLLING SHAPE

You can influence the shape of a bush by where you prune. If the leaves, and therefore the buds that grow into shoots, are in opposite pairs, removing part of the shoot will stimulate each pair behind the cut to grow.

If the leaves are arranged alternately along the stem, just one shoot will take over the extension growth, which will be in the direction the bud below the cut is pointing towards.

The growing tip of a shoot produces an inhibitor which restricts the development of the buds behind it. When you prune, you remove the growing tip and the buds behind the cut are no longer inhibited and therefore grow into a replacement shoot or shoots. Bear this in mind when shaping a shrub.

MAKING A GOOD CUT

1 This is how you should prune. Leave a very short stump about 6mm (¼in) long above a bud, angled so that moisture runs away from the bud and not into it.

2 A cut like this could lead to trouble. The long stump will be starved of sap and is likely to rot back. The rot may spread back into the healthy shoot below the bud.

BIG BRANCHES

This book does not deal with tree pruning – if you have a large tree it is best to get a qualified professional to deal with it. If you want to remove a low branch from a small tree or from a large, old shrub follow the steps.

1 To avoid the weight of a large branch tearing the wood and perhaps damaging the main stem, cut it off in three stages. First make an upward saw cut about half way through the stem, or until the saw begins to bind.

3 Avoid cutting too close to the bud: physical damage may be caused or infection could be introduced.

4 Blunt secateurs (pruning shears) or careless use may bruise or tear the stem instead of cutting through it cleanly. This is an invitation for disease spores to enter. The stump is also too long.

5 If the cut slopes downwards towards the bud, the excessive moisture that may collect in the area could cause the stem to rot.

6 Shrubs with opposite leaves should be treated in a different way to those with leaves that form an alternate leaf arrangement. Cut straight across the stem, just above a strong pair of buds.

2 Next, saw downwards a short distance further out along the branch to remove it. If it does fall, the tear should not reach beyond the first cut.

3 Finally, saw right through the branch again at the point you want to cut back to. This will be a clean cut because there is no weight pulling on it.

NEW WOOD OR OLD?

Pruning instructions often refer to old or new wood. Although the appearance varies according to the time of year, you can usually tell whether wood is old or new by the colour as well as the thickness. New wood is paler and more supple. Old wood is darker and more rigid. Study the stems on a number of shrubs - you will begin to identify each year's growth by its appearance. This is easier to do in late summer when the differences are clearer.

Above: *This year's growth – greener and flexible.*
Last summer's growth – darker and less flexible.
Two-year-old wood – darker, thicker, and more rigid.

Your Tool Kit: 1

Good tools always make a difference, and this is especially so with cutting tools. Sharp, quality blades make the physical job easier, and also cause less damage to the plant tissue. You won't need all the pruning tools suggested in these and the next two pages, unless you have a very large garden and do a great deal of pruning. Most of us can manage with a good pair of secateurs (pruning shears), long-handled pruners (loppers or lopping shears) and hand (hedge) shears if you have a hedge to cut. There are times, however, when the more specialist tools are required, and what your tool shed contains should reflect the amount and type of pruning that you expect to do.

RIGHT TOOL FOR THE JOB

Do not try to cut branches thicker than the tool is intended for. It will be hard work and may damage the tool. Manufacturers sometimes give a maximum diameter of branch the tool is suitable for. Do not exceed it.

Most secateurs will cut a branch up to 12mm (½in) thick. Long-handled pruners will sometimes cope with stems up to 2.5cm (1in) thick. For anything thicker than this, use a saw.

As dead branches are tougher than living ones, do not attempt to cut dead wood more than half the suggested maximum diameter.

IF YOUR GRIP IS WEAK

Look for ratchet secateurs if you find ordinary secateurs difficult to grip. The ratchet device enables you to cut through the shoot in several small movements that require less effort. They are worth paying a little more for.

BYPASS SECATEURS (PRUNING SHEARS)

In some countries this type may be known as hook and curved blade pruning shears and this explains the action well. A sharpened convex blade cuts against a broad concave or square blade. The hooked blade helps to hold the branch while the curved blade cuts against it.

This is the preferred type for general use, provided you keep the blades sharp. Bypass secateurs (pruning shears) usually cut cleanly, and the curved tip can be easier to get into a tight space.

ANVIL SECATEURS (PRUNING SHEARS)

With these, a straight blade cuts against a flat anvil, often with a groove in it to encourage sap to run away. The anvil is made of a softer metal than the cutting blade to reduce the blunting effect. If you don't keep the blade

Above: *Anvil secateurs.*

sharp there can be a tendency to crush the stem rather than cutting cleanly.

LONG-HANDLED PRUNERS (LOPPERS OR LOPPING SHEARS)

These are needed for thick stems, like those often found on old shrubs, or for pruning large prickly shrubs like shrub roses. For very thick stems, however, you will need to use a saw.

There are both anvil and bypass

(hook and curved blade) types, and again you may prefer to consider a ratchet type if you find the physical effort difficult.

TREE PRUNERS (TREE LOPPERS OR POLE PRUNERS)

For tall shrubs, these will make the job easier. Long-handled pruners do not reach as high and can be tiring to use above shoulder level.

The actual mechanism by which these work varies with the make. Some are operated by rope; some by metal rods; some have fixed handles, others have telescopic ones. But they all transfer the cutting action to the cutting head by a lever mechanism from the handle. A hooked end makes it easier to position and steadies the tool while cutting. Some can be fitted with a saw attachment to enable branches that are too thick to cut with a normal blade to be sawn through.

PRUNING KNIVES

Some professionals can use a pruning knife as easily as secateurs, but for anyone pruning just occasionally, a knife is not a good choice. It must be used with care.

Pruning knives usually have a curved blade because this makes it easier to ensure the blade cuts into the shoot as you cut towards yourself with a slicing motion.

Some pruning knives have attachments for budding, but these are specialist tools that most amateurs will never use.

Left: *Long-handled pruners are useful for when you are pruning large shrubs with thick stems, or very prickly plants.*

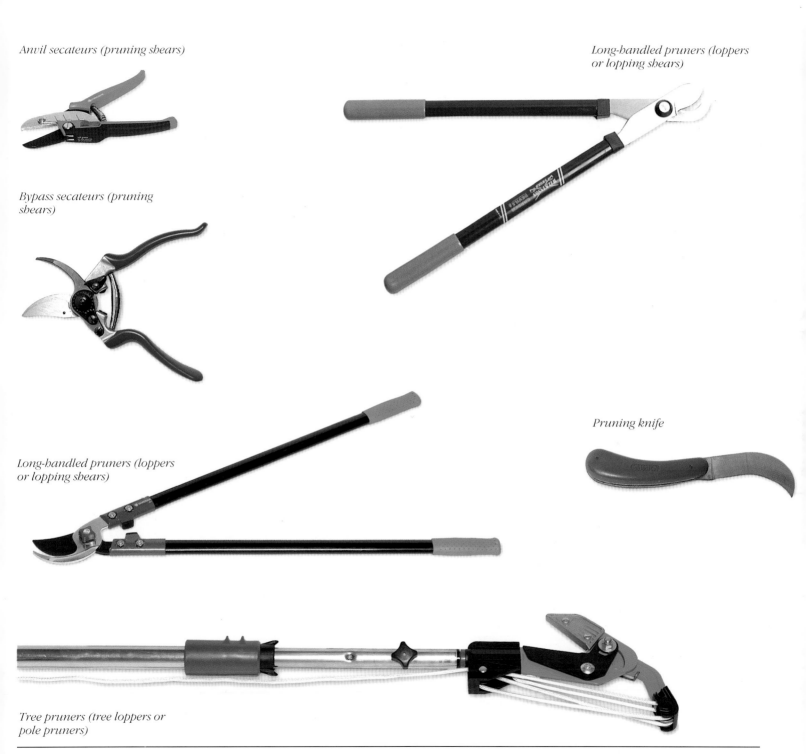

Anvil secateurs (pruning shears)

Long-handled pruners (loppers or lopping shears)

Bypass secateurs (pruning shears)

Long-handled pruners (loppers or lopping shears)

Pruning knife

Tree pruners (tree loppers or pole pruners)

Your Tool Kit: 2

GRECIAN SAW

If you want to make do with just one pruning saw for general-purpose pruning tasks, this is the best choice.

The blade is curved and also narrows towards the tip, which makes it ideal to work with in a confined space, such as among congested branches.

It is also easy to use above head height because the backward-pointing teeth cut on the pull stroke.

Variations come with a folding handle, and these can be safer to carry around.

STRAIGHT PRUNING SAW

This is a general-purpose pruning saw. Some types have fine teeth, which makes sawing hard work. Avoid those with teeth on both sides of the blade as these can accidentally damage branches to be retained. One with a blade that folds into the handle is a good idea if you have to carry it around the garden a lot.

BOW SAW

This takes its name from its shape, which is like an archery bow. Because the blade cuts on both the push and pull strokes it will cut fast, but this saw is difficult to use in a confined space. It is designed for cutting through thick branches, over say 10cm (4in).

TRIMMING TOOLS

If you have a long hedge, a powered hedge trimmer will be your most important pruning tool. It will save you the most time and effort. For a very small hedge, and for shaping shrubs and deadheading those with masses of flowers such as heathers, there is no substitute for hand (hedge) shears.

HAND SHEARS

The best shears for you are those that feel comfortable to hold and use, but for cutting performance it is the quality of the blades that matters, and, of course, how sharp you keep them.

Straight-bladed shears are perfectly satisfactory for most jobs around the garden, but some people prefer blades with a wavy edge (this helps to trap and hold the shoots while cutting).

Some have a notch in one blade towards the handle – this is for cutting through shoots that are otherwise a little too thick to cut with normal hand shears.

Above: *Hand shears with a notch in the blade can be useful for getting a good grip when cutting through thick branches.*

POWERED HEDGE TRIMMER

These come in many shapes and sizes, powered by electricity (mains or battery) or petrol (gasoline).

If you have a hedge that is too remote from a power supply to make an electric model feasible, a petrol (gasoline) version is the answer. These are also generally more powerful and can be a good choice anyway if you have a lot of hedges to cut. But they have a downside: they are heavy and more difficult to use, noisier and can be smelly.

For most small gardens, an electric version is the best solution. Mains electricity is the preferred option, but for a small or remote hedge you can try a battery-powered model. The charge may not last long enough for a long hedge, but you simply plug the trimmer in to be recharged.

Below: *A hedge trimmer.*

THERE IS A KNACK

Use a powered hedge trimmer with a wide, sweeping action, keeping the blade parallel to the hedge. Use horizontal or upward strokes rather than downward, to reduce the risk of cutting through the cable.

Even if your tool has cutting blades on both sides, you will probably find it easier to use in one direction only.

Wear gloves to protect your hands from stray shoots, goggles to protect your eyes, and do not forget that your ears will benefit from ear protectors.

Place the cable over your shoulder, tucked into a belt, so that there is no loose wire near the blades. As with all mains-powered tools, always use according to the manufacturer's instructions (not during or just after rain for instance), and protect yourself with a residual current device (RCD).

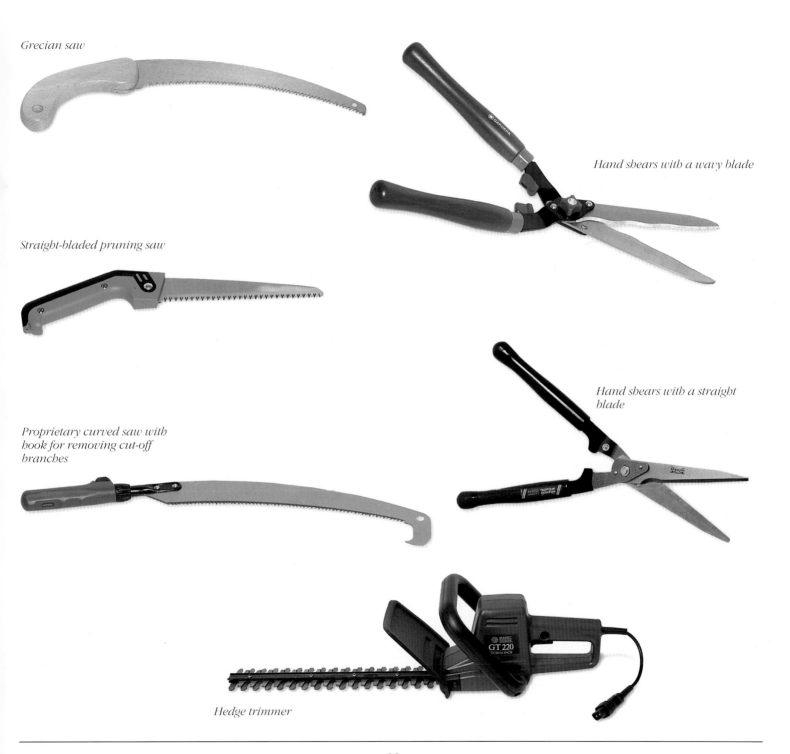

Grecian saw

Hand shears with a wavy blade

Straight-bladed pruning saw

Hand shears with a straight blade

Proprietary curved saw with hook for removing cut-off branches

Hedge trimmer

Prune Out the Problems

Even if you do not prune to shape or restrict a shrub, or to improve its flowering, it makes sense to prune out any potential problems. For instance, rubbing or badly placed branches are always best removed, and signs of rot in a branch or shoot are always best removed before the problem has a chance to spread to healthy parts. That seemingly harmless single green shoot on a variegated plant may, if left, gradually dominate the growth and the pretty variegated effect will be lost. This kind of pruning is best done as part of an annual check on all your shrubs, whether or not you usually prune them.

DEAD OR DYING SHOOTS

Above: *Shoots that are obviously dead or badly diseased on an otherwise healthy-looking plant should be cut out. They will not grow and will mar the beauty of the shrub. Leaving dead growth on the plant may also encourage or harbour diseases. Cut back to healthy wood, right back to the main stem if necessary.*

BADLY CROSSING OR RUBBING SHOOTS

Above: *Cut these out while they are still young, otherwise friction will damage them and may let in disease spores. They may also make the bush look congested if not removed. Straggly old shoots should also be cut out if they are badly positioned.*

REMOVE DIE-BACK

Above: *Die-back is a descriptive term. Shoots, often relatively young ones, start to die back from the end, slowly spreading towards healthy growth. To stop it spreading, cut back to just above a bud on a healthy, unaffected part of the stem.*

STOP THE ROT

Above: *Other rots and diseases should be cut out. Whether the trouble appeared on live or dead wood, cut it out before it can spread.*

MAKE GOOD WINTER DAMAGE

1 Shrubs of borderline hardiness may be damaged but not killed by a cold winter. Often it is biting winds rather than low temperatures alone that cause the damage, with the younger growth at the tips of the shoots browned or even killed.

2 In spring cut out cold-damaged shoots. Often you need to remove the affected tip only. This will improve the appearance and new growth will soon hide the gaps.

3 Once the damaged shoots have been removed, the shrub will soon recover.

DON'T BE A SUCKER

Remain alert to the problems that suckers can cause. These only affect plants grafted on to a different rootstock – roses and lilacs are common examples. A sucker is a shoot that arises from the rootstock, usually from below ground level; it will normally have leaves that look different (in the case of roses the colour may vary and there may be more leaflets), but with plants such as rhododendrons and lilacs you may not recognise a sucker until a shoot produces an inferior flower.

If you allow suckers to remain they will often dominate the plant over time, at the expense of the desirable variety. Cut them right back to their point of origin. This will involve pulling back some of the soil.

DON'T BE PLAIN

Left: *Check variegated plants to make sure they are not "reverting" (producing shoots with all-green leaves). If you leave these on the plant, they will gradually dominate it because they are normally more vigorous. Cut them back to their point of origin. With a few plants, such as* Elaeagnus pungens '*Maculata*', *the variegation on new shoots only develops fully as the leaves age, so be careful not to be premature with your pruning.*

Pruning for Colourful Stems

Winter colour is always valuable, and as flowers are scarce it makes sense to grow a selection of shrubs with bright and colourful stems. Dogwoods (*Cornus sibirica* and *C. alba* varieties for example) and some of the willows, like *Salix alba vitellina* 'Britzensis' (syn. *S. alba* 'Chermesina'), are widely used for this purpose. It is the young stems produced the previous summer that are the most colourful, so if you do not prune regularly the results can be dull and disappointing. This is a job to do annually in early spring or at least every alternate spring if you are not prepared to feed and mulch the plants annually to help them cope with the severe treatment.

1 This is what the shrub will look like if pruned the previous spring. If it has not been pruned for a few years, there will be thicker and duller older stems as well as the bright ones, but prune old and recent stems alike.

2 Pruning is simple but severe. Cut the stems back to within a few centimetres or inches of the stump of old wood, or to within 5-8cm (2-3in) of the ground if an old framework has not yet been established.

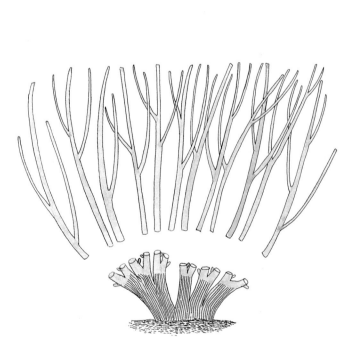

Above: Cut off the most recent growth just above a bud, close to the stump of the old, thick woody base.

3 You do not have to be precise about the length of stem to leave, but aim for about 5cm (2in). The older wood will be darker, and the shoots produced the previous summer will be brighter. Cut back just above the old wood, to an outward-facing bud if possible to give the shrub a better shape.

4 The treatment may look alarming, but new shoots will probably start to grow within weeks and by the end of summer they will probably be 1.2-1.8m (4-6ft) long. It is a good idea to hoe in a fertilizer around the base of the plant, then water well if dry, and top with a thick mulch. This will encourage very strong growth.

SHRUBS TO TRY

Shrubs to cut back hard each spring or every second spring include:
Cornus alba varieties
Cornus stolonifera varieties
Salix alba vitellina 'Britzensis' (syn. *S. alba* 'Chermesina').

Right: Cornus stolonifera *'Flaviramea' is grown mainly for its colourful stems, which can be seen at their best in winter after the leaves have fallen.*

EARLY YEARS

Do not prune a young plant as severely as described here. Allow the plant to grow naturally for a season after planting, then the following spring prune to within 5cm (2in) of the ground. This will produce a bushy plant in future years, which can then be pruned as described.

Below: Salix alba vitellina *'Britzensis' in full glory.*

POLLARDING

Pollarding creates a similar effect to that described for dogwoods. Pollarding is a form of coppicing, but on a short trunk usually 1.2–1.8m (4–6ft) tall.

2 Cut back the stems to very short stubs, leaving perhaps one or two buds on each stem to grow. The treatment looks drastic, but a mass of new shoots will be produced during the summer. These will create a colourful effect during the winter. If possible, feed after pruning, and mulch if the tree is not growing in a grassed area.

1 Once a trunk of appropriate height has been created, a head like this can be formed. This is Salix alba vitellina 'Britzensis' (syn. *S. alba* 'Chermesina').

Cutting Back to a Framework

If you've wondered why your butterfly bush, *Buddleja davidii*, has a few flowers far above head level on a tall, straggly plant, yet your neighbour has plentiful flowers on a compact plant which blooms at eye level, it is all because of the pruning. Shrubs that flower on shoots produced in the current year will become increasingly straggly year on year, with the blooms less accessible as the new growth on which they flower extends skywards. If you cut these shrubs back hard in early spring, they will still bloom, but on the new shoots produced closer to ground level. This is a really easy technique, so try it and see the improvement.

Above: *Prune back hard to just above the framework of old, darker and harder wood. This will encourage new shoots and compact growth.*

1 These old stems show how much growth can be made in a season on a plant that was pruned the previous spring. Some of the dead flower heads are still visible, showing how they flowered on compact plants.

2 Simply cut back all the previous summer's growth to within about 5cm (2in) of last year's stem. Do not worry if this seems drastic. The plant will soon produce vigorous new shoots to replace the ones you are cutting out.

3 Cut back to just above a bud. Keep to outward-facing buds as much as possible to give a bushier effect. Most of the shoots should be cut back to within about 5cm (2in) of the base of last year's growth, but if the bush is very old and congested, cut out one or two stems close to ground level. This will avoid the plant becoming too congested.

4 This is what a plant that has been cut back to a low framework of old stems looks like. Try to keep the height after pruning to about 90cm (3ft) or less.

Left: *You can create even shorter plants by cutting the old stems back close to the ground. The plants usually grow readily from new shoots produced at the base. They may already be visible if you delay pruning until early spring. The pruning can be done at any convenient time during the dormant season, but late winter and early spring are popular times.*

Below: Buddleja *in full glory. The new shoots grow fast, and within months they should be as tall as this and blooming prolifically. They are much more attractive than sparse flowers on a leggy plant.*

START YOUNG

It can be difficult to improve a very old and neglected plant, although you could try cutting it back to a few centimetres or inches above the ground to see whether it will shoot from the base. It is much more preferable, however, to start pruning a bush from an early age so that it never becomes too woody and neglected. You can start using the technique in the first spring after planting.

SHRUBS TO TRY

Shrubs that respond well to this hard pruning are:
Buddleja davidii
Hydrangea paniculata
Sambucus racemosa 'Plumosa Aurea'.

Above: Sambucus racemosa *'Plumosa Aurea' is grown mainly for its foliage. Harsh pruning in spring will result in a display like this by midsummer.*

Cutting to the Ground

Even the most hesitant of pruners can use this technique with confidence. You simply cut everything down to the ground! The technique is used only for a few plants, most notably those with cane-like shoots that rise from the ground. Some twiggy shrubs that flower on new growth, such as hardy fuchsias, can be treated this way. Although shrubby, their growth pattern then resembles that of an herbaceous plant.

SUITABLE SHRUBS

Groups of plants that can be treated in this way include ceratostigmas, hardy fuchsias and *Spiraea japonica* (syn. *x bumalda*). In mild areas, these plants form a woody framework of shoots that survive the winter but are often tidier if cut back. In cold areas the top growth may be killed, in which case the old shoots are cut back to ground level in spring. New shoots grow from the base and quickly produce a very bushy and compact plant.

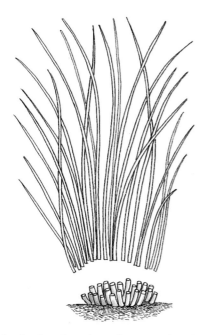

Above: *Cut back to just above the ground each spring.*

1 *Rubus cockburnianus* is among the plants pruned using this technique. It is cut back to the ground annually to prevent the growth becoming an impenetrable tangle. The white bloom on the stems is also more pronounced on young stems, so the plant is more attractive if all the canes have been produced in the current year.

2 Simply cut the old canes to just above the ground. The height is not critical as new shoots will grow from the base. Although pruning does not come simpler than this, with this thorny plant it is not without hazards. Protect your hands by wearing strong gloves.

3 You may find it easier to use long-handled pruners (loppers). Do not worry about trying to cut back to a bud as new growth will come from the base.

4 Little will be visible but if you prune in spring, new shoots will appear within weeks.

Left: *By the end of the growing season, the new shoots will be as long as those removed in the spring. And because they are young, the white bloom will be particularly pronounced.*

Deadheading with Shears

Deadheading (removing the old flowers that have died) can become a form of pruning. The technique is mainly used for heathers but, as you must avoid cutting into old wood, it is most effective if you adopt this method at an early stage. If you wait until the plants become old, straggly and woody, shearing them will not restore them to their former beauty.

1 When the flowers die trim them back with shears. Wait until spring, however, before you prune winter-flowering heathers.

2 Shear the dead heads off just below the bottom of the flower spike. Cut below the old flower head, but above old, hard wood. Heathers do not grow easily from hardened wood, so you may be left with bare or sparse patches if you cut into this.

3 The appearance will be improved as soon as the deadheading has been done, and as soon as new shoots start to grow the plant will look less manicured and more natural.

Below: *As long as you prune to keep the plants compact, with lots of new growth you should have a neat heather bed that will provide a carpet of colour.*

Above: *Clip off the dead flowers, being careful not to cut back into dark, old wood.*

SECATEURS (PRUNING SHEARS) OR HAND (HEDGE) SHEARS?

The advantage of using hand (hedge) shears is speed and convenience, especially if you have a whole bed of heathers. Pruning a bed of heathers with secateurs (pruning shears) can be extremely tiring, especially if you have to crouch down to do it. If, however, you have just a few heathers, it is a good idea to use secateurs because they leave the plants with a less "shaved" appearance.

Shaping with Shears

Lots of small-leaved evergreens can be clipped to shape. They will thrive without any regular pruning, but they can soon outgrow their allotted space. Trimming them with shears leaves them looking formal but the natural shape returns quite quickly.

3 Trim off as much as necessary of the new growth, but avoid cutting back into the old, darker wood.

4 For a few weeks, the pruned shrub will look as though it has had a haircut, but in a surprisingly short time it will regain a more natural appearance.

1 Formally shaped plants should be clipped as soon as they look untidy, which may mean doing it more than once a year. If the plant simply needs restraining, the best time is from mid-summer onwards.

2 Clip the plant like a hedge if you want a formal shape, and less severely if you simply want to restrain its growth a little.

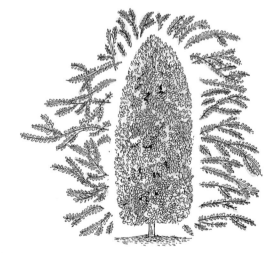

Above: *Cut off new growth but do not cut back into the older wood.*

Above: *If you make sure the growth does not get out of hand, and the basic shape is retained, evergreens will always look good, even in a small garden.*

SHRUBS TO TRY

Berberis (evergreen types)
Buxus sempervirens (box)
Ligustrum ovalifolium 'Aureum'
Lonicera nitida
Osmanthus x burkwoodii

Restraining Large-leaved Evergreens

The majority of evergreen shrubs grow happily without any routine pruning. However, if you have a small garden, you may want to restrict their size. Small-leaved evergreens can be clipped with hand (hedge) shears, but for large-leaved kinds use secateurs. Spring is a good time for non-flowering evergreens. Prune flowering kinds after flowering.

3 If you find particularly badly placed stems, crossing and rubbing against each other, cut one out.

Above: *Your shrub should not look radically different after its annual tidy up.*

1 Most large-leaved evergreen shrubs only need pruning when they need restricting, or when diseased or dead wood is found.

2 Check all shrubs once a year, and cut back the remains of the old flower heads or dead shoots to healthy wood, or to the base if this is more appropriate.

DEADHEADING

Many rhododendrons set seed freely, and this diverts the plant's energy resources needlessly.

Unless the seed is required, deadhead the plants as soon as the flowers fade.

1 The old flower truss should snap off easily between finger and thumb.

2 The developing flower bud may already be visible.

Left: *Large-leaved evergreens require little shaping, but it is worth checking the plants annually to remove dead or badly positioned branches. Removing flower heads will also improve the appearance.*

The "One Third Method"

This simple technique replaces a number of more complicated methods that can be used for a wide range of flowering plants. It is not necessarily any better, but it is a simple one to remember and easy to apply. And because no shoot is more than three years old, the method also ensures reasonably compact plants with vigorous, healthy growth that usually blooms best. Timing is easy to remember too: just do it as soon as possible after flowering is over.

1 The best time to prune using the one third method is soon after flowering has finished. This forsythia is ready for pruning and, because it is spring-flowering, plenty of replacement shoots will grow during the summer.

2 Count the number of main stems, then decide which third look the oldest (they will usually be the thickest and darkest). You do not have to follow the numeric formula slavishly, and one or two stems either way will make no difference.

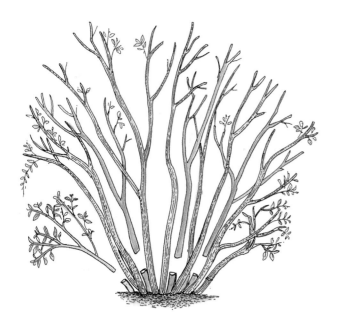

Above: *Cut out one third of the oldest stems close to the base as soon as flowering has finished.*

3 Cut back to just above the ground if the branches appear to rise from ground level, or to a stump near the base if your shrub forms a framework of thick old wood at the base. If possible, cut just above a new shoot arising from a position near the base of the plant. If there are few very old stems, make up the number to be thinned out by removing very weak ones or badly placed branches that are making the centre of the bush congested.

4 The bush will probably look a little sparse after pruning, but the basic shape and size will have been retained. Any apparent gaps within the bush will soon be filled in by new growth.

Left: *If you prune annually using this method, you will create a shrub that always has plenty of relatively young wood that will bloom well regardless of whether your shrub flowers on new wood or year-old shoots, and it should remain compact. Forsythias will remain compact and clothed with flowers from top to bottom.*

SHRUBS TO TRY

Above: Kolkwitzia amabilis *can be pruned by the one third method after flowering if you want to keep the bush compact.*

Cornus (those grown for foliage effect, such as *C. alba* 'Elegantissima' and 'Spaethii')
Cotinus coggygria (for flowers and foliage)
Forsythia
Hypericum (border kinds grown for flowers)
Kerria japonica
Kolkwitzia

Leycesteria
Philadelphus
Potentilla (shrubby type)
Ribes sanguineum (flowering currant)
Spiraea (spring-flowering species such as *S. x arguta* and summer-flowering kinds that bloom on old shoots such as *S. vanhouttei*)

DON'T START TOO YOUNG

Although the one third method of pruning is satisfactory for established shrubs, it is unsuitable for young plants. Wait until the shrub has been established for three years before you start using this technique.

Shorten New Growth

Brooms and genistas usually become too tall or leggy if you do not prune them regularly from an early age. Annual pruning once the flowers have faded will keep them looking good year after year.

Above: *Some plants, such as brooms, will become tall and leggy if you do not prune them annually, but they do not grow easily from old wood. Shorten the youngest, greenest lengths of shoot by about half, after flowering has finished.*

1 The best time to prune brooms and genistas is as soon as possible after the flowers have faded. This allows plenty of time for the new growth to develop through the summer to flower next spring.

2 Shorten the growth that was formed last summer by about half. You should be able to identify last summer's growth easily because it will be paler and more supple than older wood.

3 Avoid cutting back into dark, older wood, as new shoots are seldom produced from this. Cut the most recent growth – that made last summer.

4 From a distance the difference after pruning will not be obvious, but it should be neater and more compact. The real benefit will be cumulative, however, as the plant will become less sparse and leggy over time.

START YOUNG

Do not wait until your broom is tall and woody before pruning. This method will only work if you start while the plant is still young. It is difficult to rejuvenate an old broom that is already tall and sparse. It is better to replant with a new one and care for it as described here.

Left: *This is how a broom should be – well clothed with flowers over the whole shrub. If you don't prune to keep it like this, it will probably become bare at the base with the flowers high up on tall shoots.*

Shorten Sideshoots

Some popular flowering shrubs, such as sun roses, Cistus, require a little pruning after flowering to encourage more flowering shoots to form for an even better show next year. From a distance, you will find the shrubs look little different after pruning, but you should see the benefits the following year.

Above: *Shrubs that flower on shoots that grew the previous year (yellow in this illustration) should produce more flowers if the flowered shoots are cut back by two thirds as soon as flowering is over.*

1 Prune once the flowers are over. Although the shrub will probably remain well shaped even if you don't prune, it will flower even more profusely next year if you can stimulate it to produce extra shoots.

2 Decide which shoots have to be shortened. Select those that have just borne flowers, which will be softer and paler than the older wood. Cut this section of the stem back by about two thirds.

3 Visually estimate a cutting point on the sideshoots that have flowered, about two thirds along the length of the young growth, then prune at that point. If there is 15cm (6in) of growth, make the cut about 10cm (4in) from the tip. Ignore the older, darker wood.

4 From a distance the pruned shrub will not look very different after pruning, because most of the cutting back will have been done to sideshoots and not the older main stems. But it will encourage the production of even more sideshoots, which will flower next year.

SHRUBS TO TRY
Cistus
Convolvulus cneorum
Kalmia latifolia

Above: Kalmia latifolia.

Left: *By careful pruning after flowering the previous summer, an abundance of new sideshoots that carry the flowers has been produced. Although it would have looked good without pruning, you should have a better show if you do prune.*

Grey-leaved Foliage Plants

Many grey-leaved foliage plants lose their appeal if allowed to become old and straggly. Annual pruning will keep them compact, well clothed and looking good. Use the severe type of pruning suggested for Santolina only if starting with young plants; if you cut back into very old wood the plant may not recover, or its shape may be spoilt. If the plant is old when you start pruning, shorten last year's growth to within 5–10cm (2–4in) of the framework of old wood.

1 Grey-leaved foliage plants like this senecio (now more correctly brachyglottis) look their best with lots of new growth on compact plants. Provided you prune them annually from a young age you can keep them looking good. They can begin to look tatty and neglected if you fail to prune them.

Above: *If you prune grey-leaved shrubs – such as* Santolina chamaecyparissus – *hard each spring, you will be able to keep the plant compact. You can cut back into old wood provided there is a young shoot beneath.*

2 Small plants such as cotton lavender, *Santolina chamaecyparissus*, can be pruned hard provided they are not too old and woody. Early spring is the best time. If new growth is visible near the base of the plant, cut the stems back to within about 5-10cm (2-4in) of the ground.

3 Cut back to just above a young shoot or developing bud. Do not cut back into wood that is very old and thick. Try to confine this severe pruning to shoots that grew last summer. The plant will probably look unattractive and very sparse when you have finished, but within a month or two new growth will have created a plant that looks like new.

Above: Phlomis fruticosa *is one of the plants that can be pruned hard to encourage plenty of new shoots with fresh foliage. Do this as soon as new shoots can be seen near the base, and cut the old stems back to just above one of these. Aim to cut them back to within about 10cm (4in) of the ground.*

OLD PLANTS

Old plants that have become very woody at the base are unsuitable for such drastic treatment. Just cut last year's shoots back to within about 5-10cm (2-4in) long. Cut to a point just above a new shoot or promising bud.

SHRUBS TO TRY

Helichrysum angustifolium
Santolina chamaecyparissus
Brachyglottis (Senecio)
 'Sunshine'

Above: Senecio *'Sunshine'*.

Left: *Compact plants like* Senecio greyi *can look like this even after such hard pruning. If growing for foliage effect alone, remove any flowers that form.*

Rejuvenating the Neglected

If you have inherited a long-established garden, the chances are there are some old shrubs that have seen better days. Often it is best to dig up the old plant and replace it with a new one. Sometimes, however, even an old and unpromising shrub can be rejuvenated. The illustrations show how to improve a couple of neglected shrubs, and it is always worth trying similar techniques with any shrub that you like enough to want to save. If, after a season, there is no sign of new growth, then dig it up and replace it.

Above: *An old and neglected rhododendron can sometimes be rejuvenated by very hard pruning over a period of two or three years. This shows about one third of the branches cut back hard this year, a third that were cut back last year and are already producing new shoots close to the ground, and some branches not yet pruned. The unpruned branches will still be producing flowers, and by the time these are pruned next year some of the new growth from the pruned branches may be ready to flower.*

STARTING AGAIN
If a shrub has become really overgrown, or simply neglected – perhaps with dying branches – be prepared to be drastic. Some shrubs will not survive cutting down close to the ground but others will. If you would have to remove the plant anyway, it is worth a try.

1 On this shrub one of the branches has partly broken off the main stem.

2 Cut out badly placed or unhealthy shoots back to their point of origin. Sometimes this, together with shortening over-long branches, may be sufficient.

3 If necessary, saw down the branches close to ground level. Some shrubs will not survive this, but others will grow again from the base.

4 To reduce the risk of infection after such drastic surgery, avoid leaving the wound ragged. Use a rasp or knife to smooth off the edges of the cut.

REMOVING SUCKERS

1 Some shrubs, such as rhododendrons and lilacs, are grown on a rootstock that is decoratively inferior to the variety that has been grafted on to it. Often, the rootstock will try to re-establish itself and suckers will appear. These grow from the base of the plant, often from beneath soil level. The leaves may look similar, but the flowers will be different.

2 Remove the suckers as close to the ground as possible. Finish off by trimming in closely with secateurs (pruning shears).

3 If you do not take out the suckers they will take over your shrub.

Above: *Taking out the suckers will ensure that the superior flowers of the grafted rhododendron will not be taken over by the rootstock.*

Caring for Conifers

Conifers are remarkably trouble-free plants, and although some coniferous hedges require regular clipping, most free-standing specimens can be left alone. The methods suggested here are techniques for specific problems and your plants may never need attention. Be particularly careful about pruning dwarf conifers, as you can easily spoil their shape.

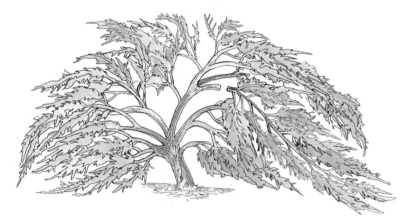

Above: *Conifers with a spreading habit may grow so wide that they begin to encroach on a path or surrounding plants. Cut back offending branches to a point where the cut is hidden by other branches growing over the top.*

■ Conifers can have two distinct types of foliage: juvenile and adult. Normally we are unaware of this, but sometimes a conifer that normally retains its juvenile form may start to produce shoots with the adult leaf form. If a shoot with a different appearance starts to grow from within an otherwise "normal" conifer, this is the most likely explanation. If left it will gradually spoil the effect of your plant. Cut out the "different" shoot, taking it right back to its point of origin.

■ Many conifers have a naturally rounded shape, so clipping one that is otherwise too large can look quite acceptable. Even a tall conifer can sometimes be topped then trimmed regularly into an attractive shape.

2 Dwarf and slow-growing conifers are sometimes planted close to paths, and in time they may grow large enough to overhang and cause an obstruction. Simply cutting the offending branches off at the edge of the path will spoil the shape of your plant. Whenever possible prune the branch back to a point hidden by the branches above.

3 Areas of brown foliage can be a sign of disease, but if it appears after a period of drought or very cold winds in winter, these are just as likely to be the cause. If caused by the weather the plant will usually recover. As many conifers do not grow easily from old wood, do not cut out until new growth has had an opportunity to hide the affected area. If new growth fails to appear after a few months of better weather, cut out the affected branch.

5 You can limit the spread of a conifer by pinching out the growing tips of offending shoots between finger and thumb. If you do this annually in spring or early summer, it will help to limit the spread. The technique is useful for dwarf conifers that are spreading beyond their allotted space.

Above: Chamaecyparis lawsoniana *Forsteckensis' clipped to shape.*

Floribunda Roses

Floribunda roses, sometimes called cluster-flowered, have many flowers open at once in the same cluster, and are noted for their prolific blooming. Although most have flattish flowers with relatively few petals, some have almost hybrid tea-shaped blooms with lots of petals and more pointed flowers. If in doubt, a good rose catalogue will tell you whether a particular variety is a floribunda.

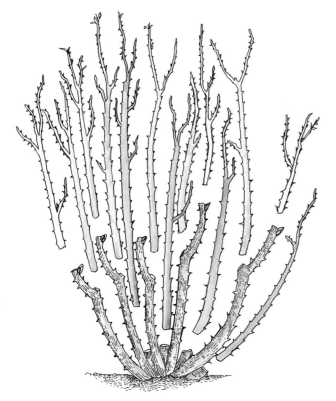

Above: *First cut out badly placed or very old shoots that are dying or diseased (shown as brown here), then shorten the remaining main shoots to about 45cm (18in), depending on the variety.*

1 Floribunda roses often look more "twiggy" than hybrid teas, regardless of how they were pruned the previous year. Do not be deterred if they appear to have a confusing tangle of thorny shoots. After you have removed unhealthy shoots just start pruning from one side and work your way across.

2 Start by cutting out dead or diseased shoots (ignore die-back at the tips of shoots at this stage, as they will probably be removed with the rest of the stem later). Cut back to their point of origin if there are plenty of other stems, otherwise to a point just above a healthy bud close to the base.

3 Next, remove any crossing or very badly placed branches. Cut out completely if necessary, or back to a bud pointing in a better direction. Also remove any very thin, spindly shoots coming from near the base.

4 Cut all the main stems back to about 45cm (18in), but use your discretion to reflect the size and vigour of the variety.

5 There will probably be some long sideshoots remaining on the main stems. Shorten these by cutting off between one and two thirds from their length. Cut back to a bud pointing outwards rather than towards the centre of the bush.

6 This is what your bush will probably look like after pruning. The framework is already well established, and new growth will soon restore the plant to its summer height.

SPREAD THE FLOWERING

Although the bushes will look less even in growth, you can extend the flowering season a little by leaving some shoots unpruned. These should flower earlier, followed by the pruned shoots. If you adopt this method, make sure you cut back the unpruned shoots next year. Do not leave any shoots unpruned for more than two years.

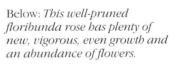

Below: *This well-pruned floribunda rose has plenty of new, vigorous, even growth and an abundance of flowers.*

WHEN TO PRUNE

Autumn and spring pruning both have their advocates. A good compromise is to shorten the height of very tall varieties by about half in the autumn, to reduce wind resistance that would cause wind-rock damage by loosening the roots. This is unnecessary with compact varieties. Most people prefer to prune their roses in early spring, but it should be done before the new leaves begin to expand.

Above: *Some floribunda and hybrid tea roses produce tall shoots that can be whipped in the winter winds, loosening the soil around the roots.*

Above: *If you want to prune in spring but live in a windy or exposed area, shorten the longest shoots by about half in the autumn.*

Hybrid Tea Roses

Hybrid tea roses, sometimes called large-flowered roses, usually have large, fully double flowers with a high centre. As new varieties are developed, the distinction between these and some floribundas is less clear than it used to be. A good rose catalogue should tell you whether your rose is a hybrid tea variety, but it does not really matter if you get it wrong. You will probably still have a good garden display whether you prune as a hybrid tea or a floribunda. In fact, you can be very relaxed about pruning both types (see Off With Their Heads).

1 Hybrid tea roses will look very different depending on whether or not they have been pruned regularly. This rose has been pruned annually and is not particularly congested. If you have a rose that has not been pruned for many years, it will require more dead wood and crossing shoots to be removed, but otherwise pruning is exactly the same. Start by cutting out dead or diseased shoots. This will make it easier to see what remains to be done.

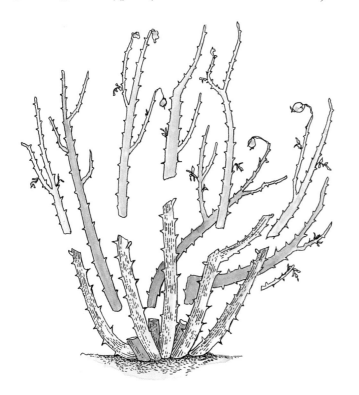

Above: *Cut out any badly positioned, diseased or dead wood (shown as brown here) close to the base. Shorten all the other main stems by about half.*

2 Remove badly placed, crossing or very congested shoots. Most of these can be cut back to their point of origin, but if growth is sparse, cut to just above a healthy bud, close to the base. Prune out or shorten any very thin, spindly shoots. If there are plenty of other shoots, cut back to the point of origin. If there are few shoots, you may prefer to cut back to about two or three buds from the base of the shoot.

3 Prune all the main stems by about half, or to within 20-25cm (8-10in) of the ground. The exact amount cut off is not critical and is a matter of personal experience and choice. Try to bear in mind the final shape of the bush. Wherever possible, prune to an outward-pointing bud to give the bush more spread rather than a very congested centre.

4 This is what your rose bush will probably look like after pruning. Although it is sparse at this stage, vigorous new growth will soon transform its appearance.

Above: *If you pruned your hybrid tea properly, this is the effect you can expect: even, healthy growth and plenty of perfect flowers.*

SUCKERS ARE BAD NEWS

Whatever type of grafted rose you grow – floribunda, hybrid tea, or patio – be alert for suckers. These are stems that arise from below the rootstock, usually from below ground level. You can usually tell that they are rootstock suckers by their appearance. The leaves will look different to those of the grafted variety, and usually there are seven leaflets instead of five.

1 Cut them off at their point of origin, which usually involves pulling back some of the soil.

2 Sometimes it is possible to pull them off.

OFF WITH THEIR HEADS

Above: *These roses were pruned with a hedge trimmer (shears).*

If you have a lot of roses to prune, simply going over the rose bed with a powered hedge trimmer (shears) will be appealing. To traditionalists it will sound horrifying. Trials of the "rough and ready" method have shown that floribundas and hybrid teas can actually produce a better display than when pruned conventionally. However, there could be long-term drawbacks: the bush may become too congested, diseases may become more of a problem due to the more congested growth and because the dead wood on each plant is not being monitored individually. For a general garden display, however, this method is well worth trying, especially if you keep an eye open for dead or diseased shoots to prune out at the same time. Although a powered hedge trimmer will save time, you can use secateurs (pruning shears) for the same kind of effect, just topping the shoots at the required level.

Shrub Roses

Shrub rose is a vague term, but it covers species of wild rose and old-fashioned varieties of bushy roses that pre-date hybrid teas and floribundas. Modern shrub roses are large bushy roses, raised in recent times but retaining many of the characteristics of the traditional old-fashioned types. Unlike modern floribundas and hybrid teas, shrub roses generally flower over a much shorter period. And most of them make bigger bushes too. They do not require such regular or intensive pruning as floribundas and hybrid teas, but annual pruning will help to prevent the bushes becoming too large or too congested.

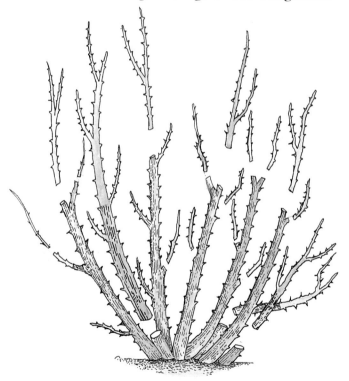

Above: *Shorten the main stems by between a quarter and a half, and the sideshoots by about two thirds. Badly positioned stems can be cut out completely.*

1 Although a rose like this will continue to flower well, pruning will help to prevent it becoming too congested and improve its general appearance.

2 After some years there will be a lot of very old, and probably congested, stems at the base. Cut out one or two of the oldest stems from the base if they have become congested or look very old.

    The rose illustrated naturally produces a lot of cane-like stems from the base; others will have fewer but thicker stems, more like those on a hybrid tea. Cut out any dead or diseased wood at the same time.

3 Shorten the main shoots (those that arise from the base of the plant, not sideshoots) by between one quarter and one half. If the shoot is 1.2m (4ft) tall, cut off 30-60cm (1-2ft).

If the rose you are pruning has also produced a lot of sideshoots (those growing off the main stems), shorten these by about two thirds. If the shoot is 30cm (1ft) long, cut back to about 10cm (4in).

4 Even when pruning has been done, you may be left with a substantial framework of stems. This is normal, as shrub roses usually make quite large bushes. With those that shoot freely from the base, like this one, you can be more drastic.

Above: *Shrub roses are usually quite large and bushy but they still benefit from pruning.*

Standard Roses

Standard roses can appear confusing to prune if you are not familiar with them. Even gardeners who are very confident about pruning bush type roses sometimes feel uneasy if asked to tackle a standard. If you concentrate on forming an attractive rounded head, however, you will have no difficulty.

Weeping standards are dealt with differently. These are pruned in summer – after flowering – and not in spring like normal standards.

1 A standard before pruning can look extremely confusing. Just concentrate on achieving a nice rounded shape while shortening the stems.

Below: *This is what a good standard will look like if pruned properly: a nice rounded head of well-spaced shoots with masses of flowers.*

2 During the dormant season (late winter or early spring), shorten the main stems in the head to about six buds, more or less depending on the age of the plant.

Do not prune too hard, otherwise you may stimulate over-vigorous shoots that could spoil the shape. Cut to an outward-pointing bud, to encourage a good shape.

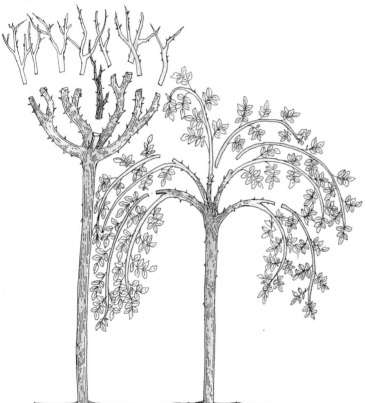

Above left: *Prune a standard rose by shortening last summer's growth by about half.*

Above right: *Prune a weeping standard by cutting back any old long shoots to a point where there is a new one to replace it.*

3 Old plants may have areas of dead or diseased wood. Cut these back to a healthy bud.

4 Shorten sideshoots growing from the main stem to a couple of buds, to stop growth becoming too congested.

5 Aim to leave a rounded head of reasonably evenly spaced branches. Although the rose looks unattractive at this stage, visualize it with the summer's growth from this framework.

WEEPING STANDARDS

Weeping standards, which sometimes have their shoots trained over an umbrella-like frame, are really rambling roses grafted on to a single stem. For that reason they are pruned in summer or early autumn, when flowering has finished, and not in the dormant season.

If you do not prune annually the growth can become congested and tangled and the head top-heavy. While you are pruning, take the opportunity to check the stake is sound and the ties are not too tight.

1 Prune each shoot that has flowered, cutting it back to a position where there is a vigorous new shoot to replace it. This is not a measuring task, as each variety and each plant will be different. Just try to visualize where a new shoot could replace the one you are cutting back. If you can't find a suitable replacement shoot, do not prune the main stem. Instead, shorten the sideshoots on the flowered stem to two buds.

Left: *Although you should have a good idea of the shape of the head after pruning, it is difficult to predict the vigour of the replacement shoots. If the growth seems uneven by spring, cut back the longest shoots to create a more balanced effect.*

Pillar Roses

Pillar roses are similar to ramblers but are grown up a post or pillar like a column. Growth is usually upright and the rather rigid stems are seldom much more than about 2.4m (8ft). They are repeat-flowering and bloom on the current season's wood. Good rose catalogues will indicate which varieties are most suitable for growing in this way.

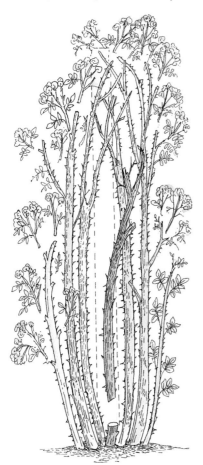

Above: *Pillar roses will only require regular pruning once they are well established. Apart from cutting out one or two of the oldest stems each year, you only need to shorten shoots that have flowered.*

1 Regular pruning by the method described here should not be done until the second year from planting. A well-established pillar rose, which can be pruned by the method described, will probably look like this.

2 Pillar roses are only pruned lightly. In late summer to early winter, shorten some of the main shoots and sideshoots from these, but only enough to maintain a well-balanced symmetrical plant. Let the shape and vigour of the plant dictate how much you prune back.

3 To stimulate the production of new shoots from the base of old plants, cut out one or two of the oldest stems close to ground level. If the growth has become too spreading, you can also remove one or two shoots from around the edge of the plant.

4 Remove spent flower trusses. This form of deadheading will also help to stimulate the production of plenty of sideshoots, which should improve flowering next year.

Above: *Pillar roses can be spectacular in a formal setting or simply at the back of an herbaceous or mixed border.*

Climbing Roses

This loose term covers plants with a wide range of characteristics, from rampant plants which will climb through a tree to restrained beauties which require coaxing up and over a pergola. Decide which group your climber belongs to, then prune accordingly.

Left: *Once-flowering climbing rose in full bloom.*

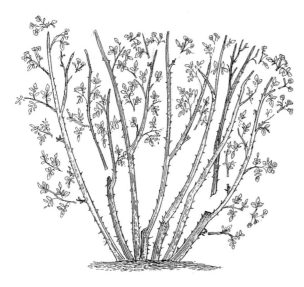

Above: *Cut out one or two of the oldest stems to a point just above a new young shoot close to the base; otherwise to a point higher up the plant where there is a replacement shoot. Deadhead at the same time.*

ONCE-FLOWERING CLIMBERS

These have a permanent framework of woody stems, usually with very few new shoots growing from the base. They should be pruned in summer.

1 Because these climbers have a stable framework of woody shoots, and are pruned in summer after flowering, they can often be intimidating to prune. Fortunately they usually flower even with minimal pruning, provided you keep the plant free of dead and diseased wood.

3 If there are strong young replacement shoots higher up the plant, prune back a proportion of stems that have flowered to just above the newer growth. Tie in if necessary.

2 Try to cut out one or two of the oldest stems each year, to increase the amount of new growth. If you can find a young replacement shoot near the base, cut the old stem off just above this. Tie in the new shoot to replace the old one. Sometimes the replacement shoot starts perhaps 30-60cm (1-2ft) up the stem, in which case cut back to just above this higher level. Do not remove more than a third of the stems, otherwise flowering will suffer next year.

4 Go along the remaining stems and shorten the sideshoots, pruning back to leave two or three buds.

VERY VIGOROUS CLIMBERS

The climbing wild species such as *Rosa filipes* and very vigorous varieties like 'Wedding Day' are not suitable for routine pruning to control their growth. Just let them have their head with a suitably robust support, such as a tree or large ropes strung between poles. In the latter case you may have to prune out some of the shoots periodically if the rose outgrows its space.

REPEAT-FLOWERING CLIMBERS

Repeat-flowering climbers generally bloom from mid-summer though to mid-autumn, although after the first flush the flowers may be fewer and more sporadic. The terms perpetual-flowering, remontant or recurring may also be used to describe these roses. They flower on new wood but, as relatively few new main shoots are produced, little pruning is required. It is best done in two stages: in summer and winter.

I When you first look at a repeat-flowering climbing rose with a view to winter pruning, do not be surprised if it seems difficult to know where to start. You will be pruning the ends of the shoots that flowered last summer. Fundamental shaping and training should not be necessary.

2 Shorten the tips if they have flowered, then go along each stem in turn to identify which sideshoots flowered in the summer, and prune each one back to two or three buds. Thin shoots that are badly positioned are also best cut out.

3 Cut out any dead or diseased wood. The basic outline of your rose may not look very different after the winter pruning, but it will encourage plenty of flowers in future years.

4 Deadhead as the flowers fade in summer, unless the plant is too large for this to be practical. Cut back to the nearest leaf.

Above: If the plant is a large one, you may not notice a lot of difference from a distance, but the pruning will encourage production of new growth that will increase the flowering capacity of the plant in the long term.

Rambler Roses

Rambler roses produce new stems freely from the base, rather than growing steadily taller on old stems. This gives them a lower and more spreading growth habit. They flower once – in mid- or late summer – and usually have large trusses of small blooms. As they flower on shoots produced the previous year, prune as soon as flowering is over.

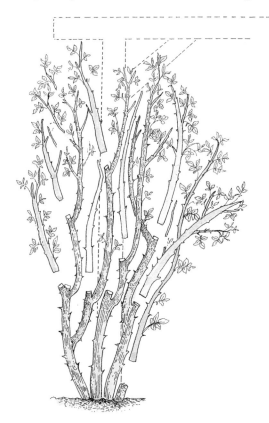

Above: *Ramblers are not difficult to prune. Cut back old canes that have flowered to a point where there is a new shoot to replace them. Very old, dying or diseased shoots should be cut out completely.*

1 Prune after flowering – late summer is a good time. Old, congested plants can be more off-putting than younger ones, but all ramblers are easy to prune if you tackle them methodically.

2 First cut out any dead or damaged shoots or those that are very weak and spindly. Do not remove very vigorous young shoots.

BARE AT THE BASE?

Sometimes varieties are reluctant to produce new shoots from the base of the plant. In that case, if there are new stems arising higher up the plant, cut back the old one to this point.

3 Cut out old spent canes that have flowered, but only where there are new shoots to replace them. Once you have a well-established rambler, try to balance the shoots that you remove with those available to replace them. This will vary from plant to plant and year to year. On old canes that have been retained (those that have flowered), shorten the sideshoots to leave two or three leaves.

4 Tie in the new shoots to the support. Wherever possible tie loosely to horizontal wires or a trellis.

Above: *Rambler roses should be pruned after flowering.*

Clematis: Which to Prune When

Clematis are not difficult to prune. Indeed some are just cut down almost to ground level at the end of winter, others are not routinely pruned at all. The problem is knowing which one to prune and how. If you get it wrong you may end up pruning out your next flush of flowers. For pruning purposes, clematis fall into three groups, and you may be able to identify which group your plant belongs to from the descriptions below. If you are still not sure, see if you can find the variety in the checklist on this page. As space is limited, only a selection of the hundreds of different clematis can be included here; if yours is not listed, ask a clematis expert or specialist nursery.

WHICH GROUP?
Does it flower in spring or early summer *and* have relatively *small* flowers?
  YES = It is probably Group 1.
  NO = Go to next question.

Does it bloom in early or midsummer, possibly with a few flowers later, and are the flowers *large*?
  YES = It is probably Group 2.
  NO = Go to next question.

Does it flower from mid- or late summer and into autumn?
  YES = It is probably Group 3.
  NO = There is an area of doubt, so consult a clematis expert or specialist nursery if you cannot find the variety listed on this page.

GROUP CHECK
This table contains some of the most popular species and varieties. If yours appears in this list it will tell you how best to prune it.

Species or variety	Group 1	Group 2	Group 3
C. alpina	o		
'Barbara Dibley'		o	
'Barbara Jackman'		o	
'Bee's Jubilee'		o	
'Belle of Woking'		o	
'Comtesse de Bouchaud'			o
'Duchess of Albany'			o
'Duchess of Edinburgh'		o	
'Ernest Markham'			o
'Etoile Violette'		o	
'Gipsy Queen'			o
'Hagley Hybrid'			o
'Jackmanii'			o
'Jackmanii Superba'			o
'Lasurstern'		o	
C. macropetala	o		
'Marie Boisselot'		o	
C. montana	o		
'Mrs Cholmondeley'		o	
'Nelly Moser'		o	
'Niobe'		o	
C. orientalis			o
'Perle d'Azure'			o
C. tangutica			o
'Ville de Lyon'			o
C. viticella		o	

Group 1 Clematis

These flower in spring or early summer on the shoots produced the previous year. One of the most widely planted of all clematis, *C. montana*, belongs to this group.

Above: *Group 1 clematis only need pruning when they outgrow their space. Just cut out sufficient branches to reduce congestion, and take those that encroach beyond their space back to their point of origin.*

1 Retain plenty of vigorous young growth like this. Concentrate on cutting out any dead, damaged or diseased shoots. Cut back to a strong bud or shoot.

2 Cut back any stems that have outgrown their space to their point of origin. Then thin out any very congested growth.

3 After pruning, the plant will look neater at the edges, especially where shoots had been encroaching, but overall relatively few shoots will have been removed. The more you managed to leave, the bigger the show of flowers next year. When thinning out congested growth, always keep an eye on the overall appearance, and try to avoid creating large gaps in the growth.

Above: *Many of the clematis in this group can be left to their own devices for many years, especially vigorous species such as* C. montana. *In a confined area, perhaps where the plant is trained along a fence or over a trellis, pruning may be required simply to improve its overall appearance and limit its spread.*

Group 2 Clematis

This group of clematis flower mainly in early or midsummer, although with some varieties, flowering may continue into autumn. Many of the popular large-flowered hybrids are in this group. The flowers are produced on shoots that grew the previous summer. Although some pruning – to thin out the growth – can be done immediately after the main flush of flowers, late winter or early spring is the best time to prune as without the foliage you can see what you are doing more easily. Pruning should not be a routine task, do it only if the plant is beginning to outgrow its allotted space.

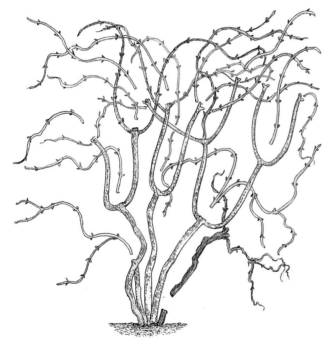

Above: *Prune when the plant has become congested and overgrown. Remove dead and damaged stems, weak and spindly shoots, and shoots that are simply making the plant too congested.*

1 Group 2 clematis will not require pruning every year, but once the growth begins to look congested some thinning can be beneficial.

2 Prune out any dead or damaged stems, and any of last year's shoots that look very weak and spindly.

REJUVENATING A NEGLECTED PLANT

A neglected or very overgrown plant can be pruned back very hard, like a Group 3 plant. Although you will lose flowers for a season, the plant should bloom beautifully the following year. And if you have trained the shoots to a suitable support, the plant will look much tidier.

3 Do not remove too many shoots. If you want the plant to cover a large area it may still be worth thinning a new plant like this, but then respacing the shoots in a fan-like formation to form a framework.

4 After pruning is a good time to respace shoots to fill in the gaps. These shoots are still young but they will thicken to form a basic framework over the years. New young growth will then fill in vacant spaces.

Above: *Prune plants in this group only when they outgrow their space or begin to look congested. If they are still pleasing and within bounds, leave them alone.*

Group 3 Clematis

Clematis in this group flower late on shoots produced in the current year, making them the easiest of all to prune. You can make a fresh start each year by pruning back severely, and the plants will be more compact and better for it.

1 Most of this growth has been made since the previous spring, and if the plant is not pruned, this year's flowers will be an extension to growth already here. This is a recipe for a congested plant – with flowers high up while the base is bare. To keep a Group 3 clematis looking good and flowering well, prune in late winter or early spring, ideally before the new leaves emerge.

2 In winter prune all the shoots back to between 23-60cm (9-24in) above the ground. This will stimulate the production of plenty of new shoots that will flower well in late summer.

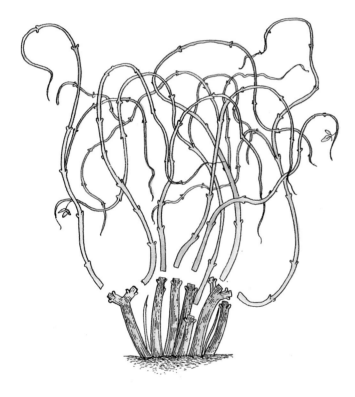

Above: *Be harsh with clematis that flower late on shoots produced in the spring and summer. In late winter, cut them back to between 23-60cm (9-24in) above the ground.*

3 Make a straight cut just above a pair of promising buds. Although the pruning height is not critical, aim for 23-30cm (9-12in) above the ground. It will not matter if you leave old stems longer, but the flowers may be that much higher.

4 Pruning Group 3 plants seems very drastic, but by early summer the new shoots will be growing fast and you should have a compact plant covered with flowers by late summer or early autumn. This plant has not been pruned back as far as some gardeners may prefer, but it will grow just as well although the flowers will be just that bit higher. On a pergola you may want the flowering stems to grow tall.

Right: Clematis 'Jackmanii *Superba' is one of the clematis that flower on wood produced in the current season, and so benefits from hard pruning in late winter.*

Pruning a Honeysuckle

Honeysuckles can be rampant climbers. Left to their own devices many will climb into tall trees to produce their spectacular and fragrant flowers. In a small garden you will probably want them closer to nose and eye level, especially if they are to cover a trellis or an arch. Young honeysuckles do not require routine pruning, but old ones benefit from rejuvenation pruning as soon as they become too congested. Late winter or early spring are good times to tackle the honeysuckle.

1 Prune your honeysuckle only if it has become too sparse at the base with the flowers far too high to smell and enjoy, or if the tangled mass of stems is too thick and difficult to manage. This sometimes happens if the plant is grown on a trellis of limited height: when growth reaches the top, the flexible and arching stems cascade downwards and may then begin to grow upwards using the already tangled stems for support.

2 Full rejuvenation pruning is drastic and you will lose flowers for a season. Simply shearing off dead or badly placed shoots, especially those beneath healthy growth over the top, will partially rejuvenate the plant. You could use secateurs (pruning shears), but the job will be very tedious among the mass of tangled stems.

Above: The twining nature of a honeysuckle makes pruning difficult, but it is only necessary to prune if the plant becomes too congested and large. Trimming back the ends of long shoots may be sufficient to control its spread.

3 If done carefully, the plant will not look very different yet much of the redundant growth will have been removed. As you will almost certainly have severed stems that remain entangled, you may notice areas of wilting or browning growth as the shoot is starved of sap. Be prepared to pull these out; sever them in several places if it helps to disentangle them.

REJUVENATION

1 Sometimes an old honeysuckle is just too congested and untidy to improve sufficiently by limited pruning. Cut all the stems back to a height of about 30-60cm (1-2ft). Some of the old stems will be too thick for secateurs (pruning shears), so use long-handled pruners (loppers or lopping shears).

2 It may be worth sacrificing flowers for a year to be able to start off again with young shoots that you can train to the support.

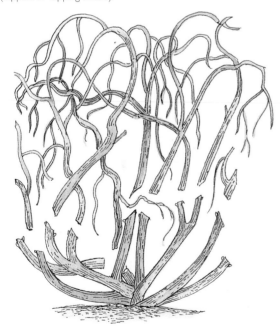

Above: *Cut the plant down to within 30-60cm (1-2ft) of the ground.*

Above: *If you prune honeysuckle hard, you will lose flowers for a season, but in the long-term you will have fresh growth that you can retrain. This drastic treatment means that the support will look bare for a while, but by the end of summer new shoots may be several metres (feet) long. Tie them in or train them to the support, to ensure even and relatively untangled growth.*

Wisteria

Wisterias will bloom freely without intervention once well established, but judicious pruning will enhance the flowering performance even more.

Above: *Wisteria may be reluctant to flower unless you cut back vigorous leafy shoots to encourage new buds to grow.*

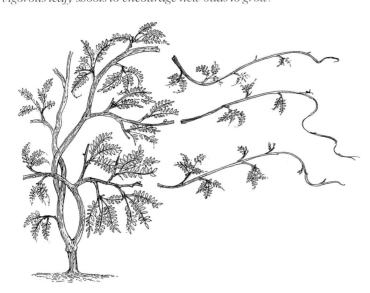

Above: *Pruning wisteria is a two-stage operation. In summer, cut back long shoots and in winter prune shoots shortened in the summer.*

1 Wisterias are big and bold, and those that are old also have very thick stems that may be firmly set around the support that they entwine. In summer the wisteria produces many long shoots. These are useful if you want to train the plant in a particular direction or to extend its cover, but for flower production it is best to shorten these in late summer.

2 In late summer, shorten the long shoots produced this year: if they are not required for further spread, cut back to between four and six leaves. From a distance you may not notice much difference after pruning, as the basic framework of the wisteria remains the same. Summer pruning serves mainly to restrict new growth.

3 Wisterias are usually pruned in two stages, the initial work being done in summer with the job being finished in early or midwinter. Shorten the shoots pruned in summer still further, this time cutting the summer's growth back to leave just two or three buds. This typically means leaving the summer's growth reduced to just 8-10cm (3-4in).

Other Climbers

Most climbers can be left unpruned unless they begin to outgrow their space. Less enthusiastic climbers, such as actinidias, *Fallopia baldschuanica* (still perhaps better known as *Polygonum baldschuanicum*, the Russian vine) and the climbing hydrangea, *H. petiolaris*, are less likely to climb to rooftop level (they do sometimes), but they still need to be controlled eventually. Spring or summer is a good time to deal with most kinds, but do not prune flowering climbers until blooming has finished.

1 Whenever possible, detach the climber from its support to make pruning easier. Cut the stems to be removed in several places and remove them in small pieces.

2 Even though it may not be possible to detach the plant completely from its support, try to unthread or detach individual shoots as you work on them.

3 Remove tough old stems that are growing behind the frame and forcing it off the wall. This will encourage new growth on the front of the trellis.

4 On old plants, remove some of the oldest stems. Cut close to the base, but above a young shoot. If a young plant must be restrained, remove sideshoots.

5 After pruning, tie in any loose shoots.

6 Although the plant will probably occupy a similar area, the growth should look less congested.

Below: *Plants like this* Solanum crispum *benefit from the treatment described here.*

Above: *When you prune climbers, remove one or two of the oldest branches, provided they are not too entwined around the support.*

Wall-trained Chaenomeles

Chaenomeles, the Japanese quinces, can be grown as free-standing bushes or trained against a wall or fence. Those grown as bushes do not require regular pruning, but wall-trained specimens benefit from annual trimming to maintain a neat appearance and prevent straggly shoots growing away from the wall to forming an untidy tangle of growth.

1 To help maintain a neat and controlled shape, tie in the new shoots to horizontal wires.

2 In spring or early summer, prune any outward-growing shoots from the main stem back to five leaves.

3 Shoots pruned back to five leaves in previous years will have produced sideshoots. Prune these back to two leaves. If growth on an old plant is very congested cut out some of the shoots completely.

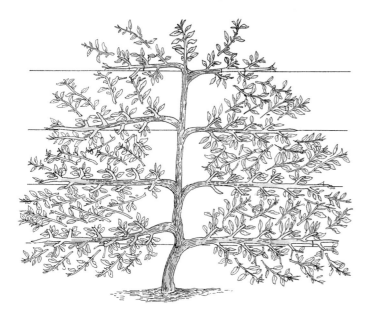

Above: *Wall-trained chaenomeles require annual pruning to prevent the new growth becoming long and straggly. Shortening the sideshoots also helps to show off the flowers. Formative pruning during the early years will have determined the basic shape of the shrub, whether fan-like or espalier.*

Above: *Regular pruning will prevent outward-growing shoots spoiling the effect. The wall should appear clothed with flowers.*

Wall-trained Pyracanthas

Pyracanthas can be grown as free-standing shrubs in a border, but they are more popular as wall shrubs. You can train them into formal shapes such as espaliers, or simply secure the stems in a more random fashion, depending on the effect that you want to create. Either way, annual pruning will help to maintain a neat appearance and avoid tangled growth that looks neglected and unattractive. Pyracanthas are sometimes grown as columns or clipped into a formal shape, usually against a wall. Although early pruning is best done with secateurs (pruning shears) an established plant can be clipped with hand (hedge) shears, just like a hedge.

1 Tie in new shoots to horizontal wires to create an espalier effect, or a fan-shaped design as shown here, or randomly with other wall fixings for a less formal style. Once the wood has hardened it will retain its shape without support, but you need to train it to the desired position initially. This is best done in spring or early summer.

2 Outward-growing shoots will spoil the shape. They can be shortened to induce plenty of spur-like shoots, but if the plant is already well-clothed with shoots, cut these outward-growing shoots to their point of origin. Shorten sideshoots growing from the main framework of the shrub to leave two or three leaves. This is best done in midsummer.

Above: *Wall-trained pyracanthas benefit from annual pruning in late spring to midsummer. Shorten the sideshoots to two or three leaves.*

Above: *Pyracanthas are grown mainly for their berries, but your wall will be smothered with cascades of white flowers in early summer.*

Vines and Creepers

Ornamental vines, such as *Vitis coignetiae* and *V. vinifera* 'Purpurea', are often grown over a pergola or a rustic framework. Unless you adopt a methodical pruning method they will become tangled and difficult to manage as the years go by. It is best to train them to create a framework of permanent branches that run along the top of the pergola or rustic frame or trellis, then prune them annually for a curtain of summer growth.

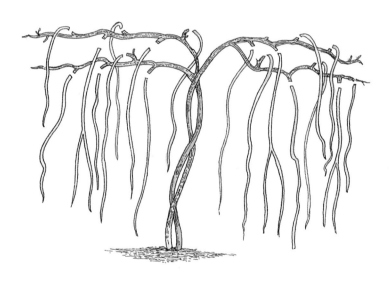

Above: *If you train a climber over a pergola or similar support, the new growth will cascade down like a curtain. Prune these long new shoots back to short spurs (stubs) each year, when the plants are dormant.*

WALL CLIMBERS

1 A well-trained climber growing against a wall will already have its framework of branches well spaced out in a spreading fan.

2 Prune last summer's growth back to about two buds from the old woody branches that form the framework.

3 Cut sideshoots from the stumps left by earlier pruning back to one or two buds, choosing one pointing in an appropriate direction.

4 After pruning, the basic framework of old, thick branches will be left, with the other shoots shortened to stump-like spurs. Although the climber will look rather bare straight after pruning, within a few months there will be plenty of new growth.

Above: *Ornamental vines put on a lot of growth each summer. If you prune them and space out the branches, they will look neater.*

SELF-CLINGING CLIMBERS

Some vigorous climbers, such as ivies and parthenocissus, may need annual constraint if they have reached the limit of their acceptable growth, for instance once they start to clog gutters, penetrate under tiles, cover windows, or spread on to walls that you want to keep clear.

1 Vigorous self-clingers such as ivies and parthenocissus can reach great heights if planted against a tall wall, but pruning is usually restricted to keeping the exploring new shoots clear of windows or areas where they can cause damage, such as blocking gutters or loosening roof tiles. They will also spread to adjoining walls if their growth is not restricted annually.

2 The actual pruning, best done in early spring, is very simple, but you may require ladders to reach the offending shoots. If necessary, pull the stems clear of the wall or support (this may require some force as they can cling tenaciously), so that you can use the secateurs (pruning shears) freely. Simply cut back far enough to allow for this year's growth. This will depend on the plant and its position, but you should have a good idea of growth rate from previous experience.

3 Although it will be obvious that some cutting-back has taken place, new growth in spring and early summer will soon soften the effect. On this wall a hard edge after pruning is acceptable, but around windows you may prefer to cut the shoots back by different amounts to avoid a clipped or straight-line appearance.

PERGOLA PLANTS

Above: *If the main shoots are trained along the top of the horizontal support until they reach the required length, subsequent pruning will be simplified. Each winter, cut the previous summer's growth back to within one or two buds of its point of origin, to keep the plant tidy and restrained, as shown in the picture.*

Above: *Over the years short spurs (stubs) will form along the main framework of branches. By cutting back to these each winter, you will have a fresh curtain of new shoots each summer without the tangled growth that would otherwise develop. If the spur system becomes too congested, cut out some of the spurs to reduce the number of summer shoots.*

Formal Hedges

Formal hedges (those neatly clipped to a regular shape) can make or break a garden. If they are well shaped and neatly trimmed they give a garden that well-manicured look. If they are uneven and poorly clipped, they will be a constant source of irritation to the perfectionist, detracting from the garden within.

Cutting a hedge seems such a natural thing that many gardeners are surprised that there is anything to explain, yet using the right techniques will make your hedge look smarter, probably enable the job to be done more quickly with less effort, and, if you use a powered hedge trimmer (shears), probably more safely too.

1 The beauty of a formal hedge lies in its crisp outline. If you neglect trimming, attention will be drawn to it for the wrong reasons. Quick-growing hedges will require trimming several times a year, but many evergreens remain respectable with one or two cuts during the year. If you are in doubt about when to trim, consult a specialist book for the best times, although you will not go far wrong if you trim whenever the hedge begins to look untidy between spring and autumn.

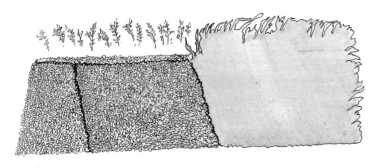

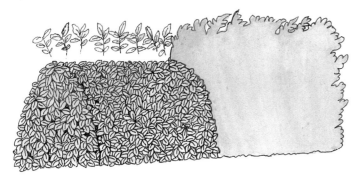

5 Try to hold the blades flat and horizontal when cutting the top. This may mean standing on steps or a raised plank.

Top: *Try to cut the sides so that they slope to the top. A flat top is easier than a curved one.*

Bottom: *A rounded top can look attractive, but you need a good eye to keep it even.*

6 Powered tools speed the job and ease the effort, but they must be used carefully. Use protective glasses or goggles, gardening gloves, and ideally ear protectors. If using mains electricity, make sure the cable is always well away from the blades, and protect the circuit, and yourself, with a residual current device (RCD). Use the trimmer with a wide, sweeping motion, keeping the blade parallel to the hedge.

2 The clippings will be easier to cope with if you lay a plastic sheet along the base of the hedge to catch them. You will be able to pick up most of them quickly and easily simply by gathering up the sheet.

3 If using hand (hedge) shears, try to keep the blades flat against the side of the hedge. If you cut with a stabbing motion the finish is likely to be uneven.

4 The most difficult part of cutting a hedge is achieving a level top. Unless you have a very good eye for this, or have lots of experience, there is likely to be a dip somewhere or a slope from one end to the other. Often you can only see this when you stand back from the hedge. The taller the hedge, the more difficult it is to achieve a level top without an aid. The higher you have to reach, the greater the tendency to create dips. String stretched taut between two canes could make all the difference. Remember to have your guide line low enough to allow for growth. It will depend on the plant used, but 30cm (1ft) below the required final height might not be too much.

7 Some conifers produce stray vigorous sideshoots, and simply nipping these off with secateurs (pruning shears) may be enough to improve the appearance between proper trims.

Right: *This carefully clipped yew shows all the graceful formality of a carefully maintained hedge.*

ROUNDING AND TAPERING

A hedge that tapers towards the top is less likely to be spoilt by heavy snowfall. If you live in an area where heavy snowfalls are common, it is worth creating a pointed or rounded top. This is best achieved over a period of time as the hedge matures. If you try to do it with an established hedge, there will probably be unattractive areas of sparse growth for some time. It is also a good idea to taper the sides, even if the top is flat. There is marginally less trimming to do (because the top is narrower) but the main benefits are to the hedge itself because more light reaches the lower parts.

Informal Flowering Hedges

Informal hedges are usually flowering hedges, so timing can be critical. If you prune at the wrong time you may cut out the flowering shoots. There is much more flexibility in the way an informal hedge is pruned, however. As a crisp outline is not expected, pruning should be aimed mainly at restricting size.

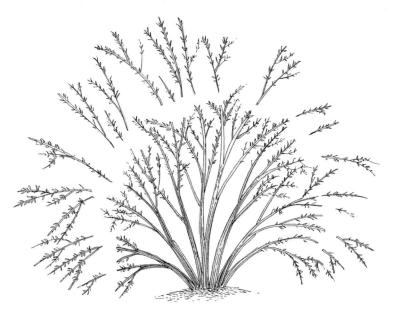

Above: *Informal flowering hedges are usually best pruned after flowering has just finished. Don't clip to a formal shape, but shorten the shoots that have grown since the last pruning to maintain compact plants with a neat outline.*

1 Most flowering hedges are best trimmed when the flowers have finished. Exceptions are where attractive fruits or berries will follow, such as *Rosa rugosa*.

4 Simply shortening long shoots each year will keep most informal hedges looking good. It restrains the size and stimulates plenty of sideshoots that give the hedge a denser appearance. An informal hedge should not look tightly clipped, so avoid trimming the whole plant uniformly.

5 Lavender is best trimmed with hand (hedge) shears in early or mid-spring, or after flowering. Shear off the old flower heads (if not already done) together with about 2.5cm (1in) of last summer's foliage. Do not cut back into older, harder wood. Rosemary can be clipped in a similar way, but wait until the flowers have finished.

2 If you have a large informal hedge, the simplest and quickest way to prune is with hand (hedge) shears or a powered hedge trimmer (shears). Only do this with small-leaved plants, such as berberis, though. Trim to size rather than attempt a smooth, even finish like a formal hedge.

3 Although more time-consuming, secateurs (pruning shears) will do a better job, especially with large-leaved plants. To restrict size, cut back over-long shoots to a position where there is a suitable replacement shoot. If there is no replacement shoot you can usually cut it out entirely. The loose structure of this type of hedge is very forgiving. Alternatively, just shorten the shoot as shown in the next step.

6 The kind of shrub rose usually used for a hedge will not require heavy pruning like those used in rose beds. If they are becoming congested and very woody, cut out some of the oldest and thickest stems close to the base.

Above: *Escallonias are sometimes clipped as formal hedges; however, if you do not clip them tightly but allow plenty of growth to remain, an informal flowering effect can be achieved. Prune when flowering has finished.*

Rejuvenating a Neglected Hedge

Hedges are much easier to manage if they are small and compact. Even if you want height for privacy, it does not have to be so wide that it is difficult to trim the top. It is often possible to cut back an old hedge to reduce its size (although conifers do not respond well to this treatment, with the exception of yew). It will take several years for the hedge to look really good again, but it could be worth the effort.

Above: *When cutting back an old, neglected hedge, do one side first. When new shoots have grown by the following year, treat the opposite side.*

1 A hedge or screen that becomes too tall or wide can take up valuable garden space, and it will make hedge trimming more of a chore. It is sometimes possible to reduce the width of an old hedge by drastic pruning spread over a couple of seasons, and it is often possible to reduce its height radically. Tackle one side the first year, the other side the following year, by which time the first side should be growing vigorously. Saw the branches back to a point less than the final desired width. Allow space for the new growth that will be necessary to clothe the stumps left after pruning.

2 The thickness of the shoots at the centre of an old hedge will probably preclude the use of secateurs (pruning shears) or even long-handled pruners. A pruning saw is an efficient way to deal with these thick shoots. On shoots that are thin enough, however, use secateurs (pruning shears) or long-handled pruners (loppers) as these are much quicker than sawing.

3 New growth should appear from the stumps, although some plants shoot from old wood more readily than others. Trim this new growth back when it is about 15cm (6in) long to encourage bushy growth, then gradually allow it to extend to the desired width. This hedge has been reduced in height and width and is now much more manageable.

Pruning a New Hedge

Shaping a hedge begins when you plant it. If you simply allow the young plants to grow to the height you want before pruning, you will probably end up with a poorly shaped hedge that is also rather thin at the base.

TRIMMING TO A TAPER

If you want to create a tapered hedge, which slopes at the sides, make several A-shaped frames from scrap wood. Position them at the ends and at intervals along the rows, then stretch string between them (nails can be used at attachment points). This will provide a useful cutting guide. Just snip off shoots that extend beyond the frame.

Above: *Shorten newly planted hedges that come as a single stem, soon after planting so that they bush out from the base. When the new leading shoots grow, shorten these too (right), to make bushier plants.*

1 If you buy plants sold specifically for hedging they are likely to be young plants with probably a single straight stem. These keep the cost down, but formative pruning is particularly important to ensure they make bushy plants. Plants like this privet should be cut back to about 15cm (6in) to stimulate low branching.

2 New shoots will be produced if you shorten the main (leading) shoot after planting. Trim these back by about half in early or midsummer.

3 Some hedging plants will be bushier when you buy them, like the ones shown here. Shorten the height of these plants by only one third.

4 Do not remove the main (leading) shoot of a conifer, large-leaved evergreens such as aucuba or laurel, or beech or hornbeam. Trim that off only when the hedge is approaching the desired height. Shorten other shoots by between one quarter and one third, to stimulate bushy growth.

FRUIT

Pruning a Dwarf Bush Apple

There are many ways of training and pruning apple trees, but for a small garden a dwarf bush is a popular option. These have a very short trunk, with branches that start close to ground level, which makes pruning and picking that much easier.

The height and spread of the tree is determined largely by the rootstock used, and this is generally more important than feeding or pruning in determining the size of the tree. Pruning is directed to preserving its shape and health, and ensuring the fruit receives plenty of light and sunshine.

There are many different techniques for apple pruning, so do not be confused if you see other methods mentioned elsewhere. To simplify things, only one method has been suggested here, but it may not be appropriate if you have a very large or neglected tree. If you have a lot of apples or other tree fruits, consult a specialist book on the subject.

Above: *Cut out badly placed or crossing branches completely or close to their point of origin. Then shorten all the sideshoots to leave a couple of buds on each.*

1 A dwarf bush apple should be compact enough to make picking and pruning simple tasks. Young trees may not need pruning. Only prune if the trees begin to look congested or neglected, perhaps with failing performance. The dwarfing rootstock will control its size.

2 Start by keeping the centre of the tree open and uncongested. Remove congested or crossing branches by carefully cutting them back to their point of origin.

3 Spur pruning is an easy technique suitable for most apple varieties. Unless your apple is one of the rare tip-bearers, shorten the previous summer's growth on the main shoots on each branch by two thirds to three quarters. If the shoot grew 60cm (2ft) last summer, shorten it to leave about 15-20cm (6-8in). On a large tree cut some back to within one or two buds.

4 Finally, shorten any sideshoots from these to leave just a couple of buds.

5 After pruning, the basic shape of the plant will be the same unless you have had to remove any badly positioned branches. The youngest shoots will have been shortened, however, and this will encourage more fruiting spurs (stubs).

Above: *Pruning is necessary to retain a good shaped apple bush.*

TIP-BEARERS

A few apple varieties bear fruit at the tips of branches instead of on spurs (stubs) along the length of the branch. The spur pruning technique is unsuitable for these. Instead, simply shorten sideshoots that are longer than 23cm (9in) and do not have a fruit bud at the tip (these are rounder and fatter than growth buds) by cutting them back to five or six buds. Do not prune sideshoots shorter than 23cm (9in).

Training an Espalier Apple

Espalier trees are space-saving and decorative. In a small garden they are often trained against wires fixed to a wall, but they do not have to be. This is a more decorative way to grow apples than as a bush or tree, but the pruning is more demanding. It has to be done twice a year – in winter and mid- or late summer. Winter pruning controls the number of spurs (stubs) and helps to ensure fewer but larger fruits, while summer pruning controls the growth and shape.

1 Once the plant has reached its final height, cut the main stem back to a bud just above the top wire; late spring is a good time. Future growth will be directed into the horizontal branches. When these have reached their limit and the tree is at its final height, like the old specimen illustrated, most dormant pruning will be to shorten the vertical growths from the horizontal branches, to encourage compact fruit-forming spurs close to the stem.

Above: *Espalier apples should be pruned towards the end of summer to control their size and shape. Cut back sideshoots to about three leaves above the basal cluster of leaves, and sideshoots from shoots pruned this way in previous years to just one leaf above the basal cluster.*

6 When the shoots are brown and woody at the base, cut back shoots arising from the main branches that are more than 23cm (9in) long to three leaves above the basal cluster. Do not count the cluster of leaves at the base. Prune sideshoots arising from the stumps left by earlier pruning that are over 23cm (9in) long back to one leaf above the basal cluster of leaves. If more growth takes place after the late summer pruning, cut the secondary growth back to one leaf in early autumn.

2 When the tree is dormant (between leaf fall and when new growth begins in spring), shorten any shoots that have grown since summer, pruning back to about 5cm (2in).

3 Shorten all other long shoots to buds close to the main stem, cutting back to one or two buds, depending on the tree and how congested it is.

4 This is what a branch will look like after pruning: no long stems but plenty of short stubby spurs.

5 Sideshoots grow vigorously during the summer, and once the wood has started to ripen (become less flexible and darker brown at the base) this must be pruned to control spread.

Left: *This is a large, old espalier, so the shape is less obvious when clothed with leaves than a younger tree would be. This shows the amount of growth made by early summer.*

Pruning Cordon Apples

Cordon apples are space-saving and more decorative than bush and tree forms, but regular pruning is essential. They must be pruned in summer and winter to retain their shape and encourage good cropping.

Above: *Summer prune cordon apples by cutting the summer's growth back to two or three leaves above the basal cluster of leaves (or sideshoots from those to one leaf).*

1 Cordons take up so little space that you can have many varieties in a small garden. And because they can be trained against a fence or wall, they do not have to encroach on other valuable growing space.

2 Prune sideshoots which are more than 10cm (4in) long, shortening them to about 5cm (2in).

3 Cut any sideshoots growing from these back to one or two buds. If there are none, do not worry.

4 Once the main stem has reached the top wire, prune back the tip to within 12-25mm (½-1in) of the old wood. Repeat annually with any new leaders that form. This is best done between late spring and midsummer.

5 Prune sideshoots from the main stem that are over 23cm (9in) long once they are mature, that is, they have firm stems that have started to turn brown. This will be in mid- or late summer. Prune back so that three leaves remain above the basal cluster (remember not to include the cluster of leaves at the base).

6 At the same time, prune back any shoots over 23cm (9in) growing from the (spurs) stubs left by previous pruning, to one leaf above the basal cluster.

Above: *This picture shows the amount of growth on the apple cordon by early summer, before summer pruning. After pruning, the surplus leafy growth has been removed, the fruits are better exposed to the ripening sun, and the distinctive angled profile is once again a feature.*

SOLVING CONGESTION

On old trees the spurs (stumps or stubs from previous pruning) may become congested. If there are too many, the quality of the fruit will deteriorate, in which case it may be better to have fewer but better quality fruit. Start thinning out congested spurs by removing those that are badly positioned, facing the wall or fence for example, and very weak ones. If your plants are still young and the spurs are not overcrowded, skip this job for a year or two.

Raspberries

There are many ways of supporting and training raspberries, but just two methods of pruning the canes. Which one is appropriate depends on whether fruits are borne on shoots produced in the current year (autumn-fruiting kinds) or the previous year (summer-fruiting varieties).

Left: *The autumn-fruiting raspberry 'Zeva' in September.*

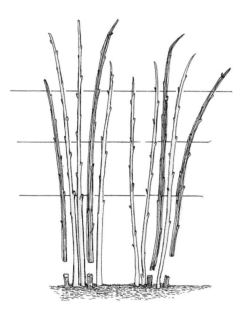

Above: *Summer-fruiting raspberries are pruned by cutting out those shoots that bore fruit the previous summer, and tying in the new canes to replace them.*

SUMMER-FRUITING VARIETIES

1 Prune before new growth starts in spring. Untie the canes from their support first so that you can remove the old canes easily. Prune out the old canes that have fruited, cutting them off just above the ground. These will be darker than the younger canes which will bear fruit next. You do not have to worry about cutting back to a bud, simply cut them off just above ground level.

2 Tie the new canes to their supports. If a very old clump has become congested and overcrowded, thin the new canes to about 8cm (3in) apart. After fruiting, tie in the canes again for next year.

AUTUMN-FRUITING RASPBERRIES

1 Autumn-fruiting raspberries are also pruned during the dormant season, but the job is even easier than with summer-fruiting varieties. Just cut off all the stems just above soil level. They fruit on canes produced in the current year, and these grow rapidly once spring arrives.

Gooseberries

Gooseberries can be trained in a variety of ways but they are commonly grown on a short leg (length of clear stem). Alternatively they can be grown as bushes that branch from the base, like the one illustrated. The main pruning is done in winter, but supplementary summer pruning is used to keep the bush "open" and well ventilated to reduce the risk of mildew and other diseases.

SUMMER PRUNING

Although summer pruning is not essential, it helps to keep the bush more open, increases the circulation of air, and thereby reduces the risk of diseases such as mildew. This is a job for midsummer. Cut any sideshoots back to five leaves from their base. Do not shorten the tips of the main shoots at this stage.

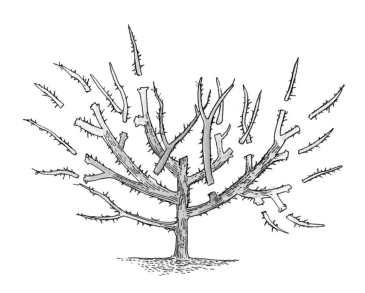

Above: *Gooseberries are not difficult to prune, though the thorns can make the job unpleasant. Shorten the summer's growth at the ends of the main stems by between one third and one half, then shorten the sideshoots growing from the main stem to two buds.*

1 Gooseberries always look difficult to prune, and thorns do not make the task any more inviting. But if you wear gloves and tackle the bush methodically it is a relatively simple job.

2 Cut out any very low, badly placed or crossing branches. Aim to keep the centre of the bush as open as possible.

3 Work over the bush to reduce the previous summer's growth at the end of each main shoot by between one third and one half.

4 Shorten sideshoots growing from the main stems, cutting them back to two buds from the old wood.

5 After pruning, the bush will retain its old shape and proportions, but the growth will be less cluttered and tangled.

Black Currants

Black currants fruit best on year-old branches, so pruning is designed to maintain a supply of young growth. This dormant-season task is best done with long-handled pruners (loppers or lopping shears), as the thick branches have to be cut off low down.

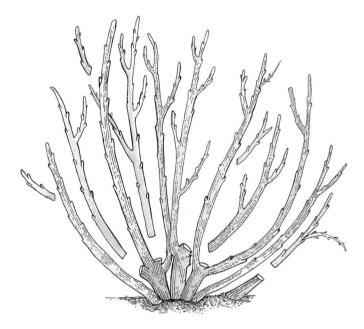

Above: *Black currants should be pruned while the plant is dormant. They fruit best on young wood, so cut out some of the oldest stems each year, close to the base where there is a younger shoot to replace it. Remove or shorten any damaged or badly positioned shoots at the same time, to keep the bush open and healthy.*

1 Black currants produce shoots from the base of the plant, and the easiest way to ensure a supply of new ones is to cut out the oldest branches.

2 Remove any badly placed branches first. These may be too low or growing inwards and causing a congested centre to the bush.

3 Next cut back some of the oldest branches (usually the thickest and darkest) close to their point of origin. In total, aim to remove one third of the main shoots.

4 This is what the plant will probably look like after about one third of the old or badly positioned branches have been removed. This is a young plant so few shoots have been removed. On older plants the shoots that are cut out will be thicker and there may be more of them. New shoots will grow to replace them during the summer. This technique ensures there are always new shoots coming along to replace the old, and no branch is more than three years old.

Red and White Currants

Although superficially similar to black currants, these plants fruit on shoots that are at least two years old, and they are sometimes grown on a leg (short single stem) as well as bushes.

Left: *Red and white currants benefit from regular pruning once they are old enough to be fruiting heavily.*

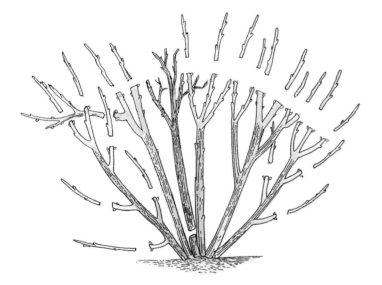

Above: *Cut out just one or two of the oldest shoots, then shorten the summer's growth by about half.*

1 This is typical of a red currant grown as a bush. Although it is a young plant, the pruning principles will be the same for an older bush, although mature stems will be thicker. Fruiting will be sacrificed if you prune when too young.

2 During the dormant period, cut out just one of the oldest shoots each year, pruning just above a bud near ground level.

3 Prune any crossing or badly placed branches back to the point of origin.

4 Shorten the wood that was produced during the summer by half: if it grew 30cm (12in) in the summer, prune off 15cm (6in). If the bush becomes too tall, prune back some of the longest branches to a replacement sideshoot that can take over.

5 Although you should not start pruning red or white currants until they have been planted for a couple of years, regular pruning will prevent older plants becoming too congested.

Blackberries and Hybrid Berries

Blackberries and hybrid berries such as loganberries and tayberries are very easy to prune. With rare exceptions they fruit on year-old canes, so all you have to do is remove those that have fruited and tie in the new ones. This is a job for the winter months, but can be done in early spring.

1 Blackberries and hybrid berries can soon become a tangled mess if you do not prune them, and tie in or train the new shoots.

2 Prune out those canes that fruited last summer. Cut them off close to the ground; you do not need to worry about cutting to a bud.

Above: *Blackberries and hybrid berries are very easy to prune. Untie the old shoots that have fruited and cut them out. Tie in younger, greener shoots that have grown during the summer to replace them.*

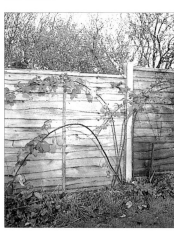

3 Untie the canes that have not fruited, and space and position them according to the system being used. Tie in new shoots as they grow.

Above: *Blackberries fruit best on one-year-old stems so yearly pruning of old stems will ensure a good crop of fruit.*

THE EXCEPTION

The blackberry variety 'Himalayan Giant' does not produce new canes as freely as most other varieties, and it crops well on canes that are two years old as well as one-year-old canes. The best way to prune this variety is to cut out those canes that have fruited twice.

Blueberries

Blueberries are slow-growing bushes that require little pruning. Because they fruit best on branches that are two or three years old, it is best not to prune them at all for the first three or four years. Spring is the best time to prune. Soil conditions are more important than pruning if you want a good crop: they must have an acid soil.

Above: *Blueberries require little pruning, but on an old plant it is best to cut out a few of the oldest shoots if they have become unproductive. Cut back to a younger shoot. Prune out any badly placed shoots at the same time.*

Above: *When pruning blueberries, cut out weak or very spindly growth. Initially this may be all that is required. On older plants, once a branch is becoming less productive, prune it out, preferably cutting it back to a point where there is a young replacement shoot. Otherwise cut it back to its point of origin. Do not remove more than a quarter of the branches. Blueberries are slow-growers, and the amount of pruning should reflect this.*

AN A-Z OF PRUNING

Pruning Checklist

Use this checklist of some of the most popular and widely grown shrubs to decide which technique to use, and when. You will find almost all the genera of shrubs widely grown in gardens, but limitations of space make it impossible to include every species and variety. Generally, however, all the most popular species under each heading can be treated as described. If there are special exceptions, especially for common shrubs, these have been mentioned. To make the book internationally comprehensible, the shrubs have been listed alphabetically by Latin name. If you only know a plant by its common name, use the index of common names.

ABELIA
Most abelias flower over an exceptionally long period because they flower on old wood, produced the previous year, and on new shoots from the current year. Prune established plants (at least three or four years old) by cutting out the oldest third of the shoots (see The "One Third Method"). Early spring is an ideal time as you can see whether any stems have been killed by a hard winter.

ABELIOPHYLLUM
A. distichum is the only species, and it flowers in spring on shoots produced the previous year. If you have to prune an old or congested specimen, cut out the oldest third of the shoots (see The "One Third Method") in mid- or late spring. This will not be required on young plants, and not even annually on mature ones. Prune only if the plant is

flowering poorly or looking congested.

ABUTILON
These can be grown only as wall shrubs or in a protected position in cold regions. In some areas they are unsuitable for growing as outdoor shrubs.

A. megapotamicum is grown against a wall. It will not require pruning for some years, but if it begins to outgrow its space, just clip it lightly with hand (hedge) shears in mid- or late spring.

A. vitifolium is grown as a free-standing shrub in favourable areas. If pruning does become necessary, shorten the sideshoots after flowering (see Shorten Sideshoots).

ACTINIDIA
The species most often grown as an ornamental climber is *A. kolomikta*, which is usually

trained against a wall, secured to horizontal wires.

Only prune when it has outgrown its allotted space. Cut over-long shoots back to within about 15cm (6in) of their point of origin in early summer, then tie in new shoots to replace them.

If the plant is becoming much too vigorous for the space, cut out one or two shoots close to the base each year.

If the shoots are cascading down from a support such as a pergola, treat like an ornamental vine (see Vines and Creepers).

Above: Actinidia kolomikta.

AKEBIA
These twining climbers are normally trained along horizontal wires fixed to a wall. No routine pruning is needed, but if the plant outgrows its space, cut out a few of the oldest shoots close to their point of origin each spring.

If necessary, prune out the growing tips of long shoots in

spring and train the new sideshoots produced to fill in any gappy areas.

ALOYSIA
A. triphylla, which is also widely sold as *Lippia citriodora*, is the plant that you are likely to encounter. It can be over-wintered outdoors only in mild areas as very cold winters are likely to kill it. Where frosts are only moderately severe it may survive with only dead or damaged shoots requiring pruning.

Wait until new growth can be seen in spring, then prune back to live wood. If the shrub eventually becomes unshapely, try cutting all the shoots back to about 30cm (12in) above the ground. If you want a bushier plant pinch back any shoots that are too long.

In mild regions the plant may be unscathed by winter and become relatively large. In these circumstances, just cut out the oldest third of the stems each spring (see The "One Third Method").

ARISTOLOCHIA
These are climbing plants, with *A. macrophylla* the species usually grown. It requires pruning only if it has outgrown its allotted space. In that case, cut back the longest shoots by about a third in spring, and, if necessary, cut out completely any that are growing in an unsuitable position and are encroaching on other plants.

ARTEMISIA
Some of the shrubby artemisias, such as *A. abrotanum* and *A.*

absinthium, will remain more compact and better looking if cut back quite hard each spring like *Santolina chamaecyparissus* (see Grey-leaved Foliage).

Other shrubby species require minimal pruning. It is usually sufficient to remove any winter-damaged shoots in midspring, and to shorten any very long shoots if the plant is becoming leggy.

AUCUBA
These slow-growing evergreens seldom require pruning. Shape or restrict growth if a plant becomes too large (see Restraining Large-leaved Evergreens).

AZALEA, see Rhododendron and Azalea.

BERBERIS
Prune only to shape or to maintain the desired size. Most berberis grown in the shrub border can be left for years without pruning.

Above: Berberis stenophylla.

If a shrub is becoming too large, start cutting out the oldest third of the shoots each year (see The "One Third Method") for three years, to rejuvenate the plant. Cut them back to a young shoot close to the base. This one third pruning is advisable annually for *B. dictyophylla*, which is grown mainly for the white bloom on the stems.

Late winter to midspring is a good time to prune most deciduous berberis. Prune evergreen species after they have flowered, which is usually in spring.

BRACHYGLOTTIS (SYN. SENECIO)
Prune back the previous year's growth to within 5-10cm (2-4in) of the framework of old woody branches in spring. Shrubby brachyglottis (senecios) will eventually look tatty and neglected if not pruned, especially after a hard winter.

If not cutting back to within 5-10cm (2-4in) of a framework of old wood, just cut out damaged or badly placed shoots.

If you stimulate plenty of new growth, the plant will always have a fresh, well-clothed appearance.

BUDDLEJA
The most widely-grown species is *B. davidii*, and this requires hard pruning each spring to prevent it becoming tall and lanky. It can be cut back very low or to a taller permanent framework, perhaps 60-90cm (2-3ft) tall (see Cutting Back to a Framework).

Many other buddlejas, including *B. fallowiana*, can be treated in the same way, but do not use this technique for species that flower on shoots produced the previous year, such as *B. alternifolia* and *B. globosa*. Instead, on large plants cut out the oldest third of the stems after flowering (usually early or midsummer).

BUXUS
This is commonly seen as a clipped hedge and as formal specimens. Over-large plants in a border can be clipped with hand (hedge) shears (see Shaping with Shears). As a border shrub, however, it seldom requires clipping. A large, overgrown specimen can be pruned hard over a period of three years, limiting the number of shoots sawn out at any one time.

CALLICARPA
Routine pruning is not required. If you do have to prune, perhaps to improve its shape, spring is a good time. Cut out old wood rather than new shoots.

CALLUNA
Clip off the old flowered shoots after flowering, but do not cut back into old wood (see Deadheading with Shears).

CAMELLIA
Routine pruning is unnecessary, but deadheading will improve the appearance of the shrub. If any shoots are damaged by a severe winter, cut back to a healthy shoot once the new growth can be seen.

CAMPSIS
This vigorous climber will need pruning only once it grows too large for its allotted space. It flowers on the current season's growth, so prune any over-long shoots back to two or three buds in winter or early spring.

CARPENTERIA
The only species is *C. californica*, and it does not require routine pruning. If it becomes too large, cut out the oldest third of stems (see The "One Third Method") in late summer. This will provide a regular supply of new shoots if you continue the technique for a few years. The plant suffers winter damage in cold regions, and if this happens cut back affected shoots to healthy growth in spring.

CARYOPTERIS
C. x clandonensis, which looks more like an herbaceous plant than a woody shrub, is the plant you are most likely to come across. You can cut it back hard to a low framework, or simply shorten the shoots to maintain a compact shape.

1 This caryopteris has formed a woody framework of low branches, so last year's shoots only need shortening back.

2 Shorten the shoots to maintain a rounded, compact shape and size. If necessary, you can prune back more severely – but do not cut back into the old, thick shoots.

CEANOTHUS, DECIDUOUS

Deciduous ceanothus tend to flower poorly as they get older unless you prune mature plants annually. As new leaves begin to appear in spring, prune the shoots back to within about 10cm (4in) of the previous year's growth.

CEANOTHUS, EVERGREEN

Routine pruning is not essential, but to improve flowering you can shorten flowered shoots by about two thirds when the blooms have finished (see Shorten Sideshoots).

In harsh regions they may suffer winter damage, but affected shoots can often be cut back to healthy shoots in spring.

CERATOSTIGMA

The growth can appear almost herbaceous rather than woody like most shrubs, and *C. plumbaginoides* can have the previous year's growth cut to just above ground level in early or midspring (see Cutting to the Ground).

C. willmottianum is taller, so shorten old shoots that flowered last year back to new shoots lower down in spring. They can be cut quite close to the ground and still respond with plenty of summer growth.

1 Ceratostigmas will look like a tangled mass of twiggy growth in winter.

2 They can be cut back to within a few centimetres (inches) of the ground.

3 Although this treatment looks drastic, new growth will soon appear to hide the old stumps.

CHAENOMELES JAPONICA

No routine pruning is required when *C. japonica* is grown as a free-standing shrub, but when a specimen is trained against a wall it will benefit from annual pruning once well established.

Prune *C. japonica* in spring when flowering has finished, by cutting back the previous year's growth to two or three buds. This creates plenty of flowering spurs while keeping the growth compact against the wall.

If the plant grows too large cut out a few of the oldest branches when the plant is dormant.

TRAINING

Chaenomeles are best trained like a fan or espalier against a wall or fence by tying in developing shoots to wires. To encourage dense, compact growth, shorten any shoots growing away from the wall to five leaves. Shorten sideshoots from these to three leaves. The best time to do this is after flowering.

CHIMONANTHUS

Prune only well-established plants that have become too large. Cut out the oldest third of the stems each year. This may not be required routinely once the bush has been brought back to size.

CHOISYA

No routine pruning is required, but in cold regions the tips of the shoots may be damaged by cold winds, leaving the leaves brown. Cut affected shoots back to healthy growth.

If the plant becomes too large, each year cut out the oldest third of the stems close to the base until it is an appropriate size. Once a good shape and size have been achieved, pruning will not be required every year.

CISTUS

Pruning is not essential, but it will often increase the number of flowers the following year. Prune after flowering by shortening back flowered shoots by two thirds (see Shorten Sideshoots), but do not cut back into old wood. Most species are reluctant to grow new shoots from old wood.

CLERODENDRUM

The species usually grown as a shrub is *C. trichotomum*, and this requires no routine pruning.

C. bungei is sometimes grown in mild regions, although it is likely to be cut down by frost. As an established plant will usually produce new growth from the base, you can cut the shoots back to ground level in spring (see Cutting to the Ground).

CLETHRA

No routine pruning is required, but if a mature plant becomes too large or dense, remove some of the oldest shoots close to the ground. There will usually be some young shoots growing from near the base to replace them.

COLUTEA

To keep a mature shrub compact, prune out the oldest third of the stems (see The "One Third Method") in late spring.

CONVOLVULUS

Prune once mature to keep the plant tidy and flowering well. Cut back the current year's flowered shoots by two thirds (see Shorten Sideshoots) in late summer.

CORDYLINE

No routine pruning is required, but remove any old dead leaves which often appear at the base once a trunk has formed so that they do not mar the effect. Do this in late spring.

CORNUS

For flowers: those grown for their large flowers, such as *C. florida* and *C. kousa*, require no routine pruning.

For foliage: varieties grown mainly for their ornamental foliage, such as *C. alba* 'Elegantissima' and 'Spaethii', require pruning only once they become too large. Then you can keep them compact and looking good by cutting out the oldest third of the stems (see The "One Third Method") in midspring.

Do not do this with the tree-like foliage cornus, such as *C. controversa* 'Variegata' which does not require routine pruning.

For coloured stems: The popular dogwoods grown for their bright winter stems, such as *C. alba* 'Sibirica' and *C. stolonifera* 'Flaviramea', will be much better if you prune very severely annually or every second year, in early spring. This encourages the production of masses of compact young stems, which have the brightest colours. (See Pruning for Colourful Stems, where the technique is illustrated.)

CORYLOPSIS
No routine pruning is required, but one or two of the oldest shoots can be cut out close to the ground if the plant becomes too large or congested.

CORYLUS
Those grown as small trees require no routine pruning. Shrubby types grown mainly for foliage effect, such as *C. maxima* 'Purpurea', will remain more compact and attractive if you prune out the oldest third of the stems each spring (see The "One Third Method").

COTINUS
Most cotinus do not require routine pruning, but some are pruned to make the most of either flowers or foliage. One of the most commonly grown is *C. coggygria*, and if you want a good balance of flowers and foliage on a reasonably compact shrub, cut out the oldest one third of the stems each spring (see The "One

Third Method"). Otherwise prune only if there is a specific problem.

Above: Cotinus coggygria.

COTONEASTER
There are many kinds of cotoneaster, and most thrive without any routine pruning. Some, especially those that spread horizontally along the ground or against a wall, will

Above: Cotoneaster horizontalis.

require regular pruning once they outgrow their space. When this happens, cut out the oldest third of the stems each year (see The "One Third Method").

Evergreen species are best pruned in midspring, and deciduous ones in late winter or early spring.

CYTISUS
Without pruning, well-established plants, especially *C. scoparius* varieties and hybrids, will gradually become bare at the base, often with flowers at the ends of increasingly tall stems.

Prune established plants after flowering, shortening growth made the previous year by half (see Shorten New Growth).

C. battandieri is sometimes grown as a wall shrub, in which case cut out any surplus branches growing out from the wall in midsummer if they cannot be tied in to fill a space. Free-standing specimens can simply have any wayward shoots cut away in spring. Otherwise don't worry about pruning routinely.

Dwarf cytisus, such as *C. x kewensis* and *C. x praecox*, do not require routine pruning.

DABOECIA
Trim lightly with hand (hedge) shears to deadhead after flowering (see Deadheading with Shears).

DAPHNE
No routine pruning is required.

DEUTZIA
These will look good even without pruning, but to keep mature plants compact and flowering well, cut out the oldest third of the stems as soon as flowering has finished (see The "One Third Method").

Above: Deutzia x elegantissima.

DIERVILLA
Routine pruning is not essential for a good display, but it will usually improve flowering. Prune out the oldest third of the stems (see The "One Third Method") immediately after flowering has finished.

DISANTHUS
No routine pruning is required.

ELAEAGNUS
No routine pruning is required, but if a plant eventually becomes

Above: Elaeagnus pungens *'Maculata'*.

too large, try cutting out the oldest third of the stems each spring for three years. Do not continue doing this unless the shrub again becomes too large.

ENKIANTHUS

No routine pruning is required.

ERICA

Most types can simply be pruned by clipping with hand (hedge) shears to remove the dead flowers (see Deadheading with Shears). This is usually done once flowering is over, but wait until spring for winter-flowering kinds.

Tree heathers, such as *E. arborea*, are best pruned by shortening new shoots by two thirds after flowering (see Shorten Sideshoots). Some tree heathers may not require regular pruning.

ESCALLONIA

Do not prune until the plant appears to be outgrowing its space or becomes too tall. Then you can prune annually by cutting out the oldest third of the stems (see The "One Third Method") in late spring, until the plant is looking good again.

EUCALYPTUS

Only specimens grown as compact shrubs for foliage effect require routine pruning. Hard pruning not only keeps the plants shrub-sized, it also ensures the foliage is of the more attractive juvenile type (adult leaves are usually more elongated).

While the plant is still young, prune back to about 30cm (12in) above the ground in spring. New shoots will soon be produced from close to the base. In future years, just prune back to within a few centimetres or inches of the old stump each spring.

EUONYMUS

There are many kinds of euonymus, but none of them requires routine pruning. If an old plant begins to look past its best, however, cut out the oldest third of the stems in spring (see The "One Third Method").

Above: Euonymus *'Emerald Gaiety'* and *'Emerald 'n' Gold'*.

FALLOPIA

Prune only to restrict size (see The "One Third Method").

FATSHEDERA

Routine pruning is unnecessary, but once a plant begins to lose its shape, try pruning out the oldest third of the branches for two or three seasons. This should improve its shape and keep the plant compact.

FATSIA

No routine pruning is required, but if the shrub becomes too large, prune out the oldest third of the stems for two or three seasons to rejuvenate it. Also be prepared to cut out any shoots that are growing at the wrong angle and spoiling the shape.

FORSYTHIA

Forsythia benefits from annual pruning, immediately after flowering. One of the easiest methods is to remove the oldest third of the shoots (see The "One Third Method").

This keeps the shrub compact as well as maintaining a good supply of young flowering growth.

F. suspensa is sometimes trained against a wall. In this case cut back sideshoots that have flowered to about two buds of the old wood, as soon as flowering has finished.

FOTHERGILLA

No routine pruning is required.

FREMONTODENDRON

In cold regions *F. californicum* is grown as a wall shrub for protection. Once the plant is well established and the size you desire, prune back by two thirds shoots that grew last year (see Shorten Sideshoots), after flowering. Be warned that the down from the stems can irritate eyes and skin.

FUCHSIA, HARDY

Above: Fuchsia magellanica.

Hardy fuchsias can be left unpruned in areas where they are not affected by severe winter frosts, but they will often grow very large. Where winters are harsher the top growth will be killed, so you must spring prune to remove the dead growth. Cut back the old or dead stems to just above the ground. Unless the winter has been severe, or you live in a very cold region, new growth will appear from the base.

1 Except in mild areas where frosts are seldom severe, the top growth of hardy fuchsias will usually be killed. Even where it is not, you may prefer to prune back hard to keep the shrub compact.

2 Cut the old shoots back to a couple of centimetres (1in) above the ground. New shoots will usually grow from the base once warm spring weather arrives.

GARRYA

No routine pruning is required until the shrub has reached its required size. Then cutting out the oldest third of the stems (see The "One Third Method") in midspring each year will keep the plant compact and vigorous.

Above: Garrya x issaquahensis.

GAULTHERIA (SYN. PERNETTYA)

No routine pruning is required, but if the plant becomes too large, cut out the oldest third of the stems (see The "One Third Method") in spring to restrict growth. Outward spread is difficult to restrict except by removing sections of root and shoots from around the edge.

If *G. shallon*, which spreads to form a thicket, outgrows its allotted space, remove pieces from around the edge. Chop off sections of the plant with its roots with a spade if necessary.

GENISTA

No routine pruning is required, but *G. hispanica* often looks better if clipped over with hand (hedge) shears to remove several centimetres or inches of growth immediately after flowering. This ensures it remains looking neat

and compact. If *G. aetnensis* or *G. lydia* begin to look straggly, cut back flowered shoots by half (see Shorten New Growth) in late summer.

GRISELINIA

No routine pruning is required.

HALIMIOCISTUS

Routine pruning is not essential, but to encourage more prolific flowering shorten flowered shoots by two thirds (see Shorten Sideshoots) in late summer.

HAMAMELIS

No routine pruning is required.

HEBE

Above: Hebe x franciscana *'Variegata'*.

No routine pruning is normally required, but if you grow species or varieties of borderline hardiness for your region it is sometimes necessary to prune out winter-damaged shoots once new ones appear. Many hebes may be killed by severe winter cold.

If a plant becomes too large or very leggy, it may be possible to rejuvenate it by cutting back hard

in spring. Some will grow again even if you cut them back almost to ground level.

HEDERA

Ivies need no routine pruning until they outgrow their allotted space. Then annual cutting back to a point that will allow for a season's growth without encroaching too far will be sufficient. This is particularly important where shoots may go beneath tiles or block a gutter (see Vines and Creepers).

HELIANTHEMUM

Regular annual pruning will help to keep these dwarf shrubs compact and flowering well. Cut two thirds off the new shoots in early or midsummer when flowering is over. It is more practical to do this with hand (hedge) shears even if the amount cut off is less precise. If you do this there may even be a second flush of flowers in autumn.

Above: *Helianthemum.*

HELICHRYSUM

The shrubby species benefit from regular pruning, which keeps

them compact and attractive.

The popular grey-leaved *H. angustifolium* is best cut back close to the old wood (see Grey-leaved Foliage Plants). If you have not done this regularly since the plant was young, it may be necessary to cut back to a taller framework of old stems. Avoid cutting back into the older, harder wood.

HIBISCUS, SHRUBBY

The popular *H. syriacus* requires no routine pruning. If the shrub becomes too large, cut out the odd individual branch to control the size of an old specimen, preferably in spring.

HIPPOPHAE

No routine pruning is required, but if the shrub becomes too large or untidy, prune out the oldest third of the stems each year (see The "One Third Method") until a better shape and size has been achieved. Beware of the thorns when pruning.

HYDRANGEA

Different types of hydrangea require different pruning techniques.

The popular mophead and lacecap forms of *H. macrophylla* require little pruning other than to remove any very thin shoots, or a few of the oldest and thickest if the plant has become congested. Concentrate on improving its shape and keeping the centre of the bush open. The old flower heads are usually left on through the winter to help protect the new buds, but these should be cut off in spring as soon as new leaves appear.

The climbing *H. petiolaris* requires no routine pruning, but if it outgrows its allotted space prune back the offending shoots to their point of origin during the summer.

H. paniculata flowers on shoots produced in the current season, and the flowers are often bigger and better if you prune back to a low framework of established branches each spring, like a buddleja (see Cutting Back to a Framework).

1 The old flower heads are usually left on mophead and lacecap hydrangeas (forms of *H. macrophylla*) during the winter, to afford a little extra protection for the new buds.

2 Cut off the old flower heads in spring when the new leaves emerge.

3 Prune just above the first emerging leaves beneath the old flower head.

HYPERICUM

Most of the hypericums grown in the shrub or mixed border require little pruning, but you can keep a mature plant compact by cutting out the oldest third of the stems in spring (see The "One Third Method").

Some grown mainly for foliage effect, such as *H. moserianum* 'Tricolor', can be pruned hard to a low framework like a buddleja (see Cutting Back to a Framework), although it is best to do this only every second spring unless you are prepared to water and feed to compensate.

The suckering ground cover *H. calycinum* is best pruned harshly every spring. Cut it down to ground level in early spring to get rid of the old growth and tidy up the plant. New growth will soon appear and will flower profusely.

Most twiggy hypericums can be trimmed back to size and shape with hand (hedge) shears in spring.

ILEX

Hollies are very slow-growing and require no routine pruning. Those clipped into a formal shape, however, are best shaped with secateurs (pruning shears) in early spring.

INDIGOFERA

I. heterantha, still widely grown under its older name of *I. gerardiana*, is often damaged in winter by frosts. If badly affected, it is always worth trying to encourage new growth from the base by cutting it down to about 10cm (4in) above the ground in midspring. If just a few shoots, or the tips, are damaged, simply shorten them to healthy wood.

Normally it requires no other pruning, but if you want to

encourage a bushier shape cut the new shoots back by two thirds (see Cutting Back to a Framework) in late summer.

JASMINUM

The proper climbers such as *J. officinale* require no routine pruning, but overcrowded shoots can be thinned out after flowering, taking them back to the point of origin if growth has become congested.

The widely grown winter-flowering *J. nudiflorum* is a sprawling shrub usually grown against a trellis or wall. On a well-established large plant, cut out the oldest third of the shoots (see The "One Third Method") each year when flowering is over. This will ensure the shrub remains compact with plenty of flowers. You can also keep the plant within bounds by shortening shoots that have outgrown their allotted space.

1 *Jasminum nudiflorum* is a sprawling plant. Where its stray shoots are an inconvenience, tidy up the plant annually when flowering is coming to an end.

2 Cut back all shoots that have outgrown their allotted space. Prune back far enough to allow for new summer growth. Also cut back any shoots growing too far away from the wall or fence.

3 This is what the plant will probably look like after pruning. By next winter it will look well clothed with new shoots.

KALMIA

Only prune once the shrub has become too large for its allotted space, then cut out the oldest third of the stems (see The "One Third Method") each year until its size is contained. Do this as soon as possible after flowering has finished, and only if the shrub needs it. A few compact species do not require any routine pruning.

KERRIA

The only species is *K. japonica*, a

common shrub that tends to look straggly if neglected. Prune out one third of the stems (see The "One Third Method") after flowering, which usually means in early summer. As the plant spreads outwards, it may be necessary to chop off pieces around the edge with a spade to restrain its spread.

Above: Kerria japonica *'Pleniflora'*.

KOLKWITZIA

The only species is *K. amabilis*, and no routine pruning is required. If you want to keep a large shrub compact, cut out the oldest third of the stems (see The "One Third Method") as soon as flowering has finished.

LAURUS

L. nobilis is sometimes grown as a border shrub, but is also grown as an ornamental herb in large pots or tubs, or as a centrepiece in a herb garden. Plants are sometimes trained into formal shapes, but this requires special skills and patience.

A free-standing shrub in a border is unlikely to require any routine pruning.

Clip pot-grown and formally shaped specimens with secateurs (pruning shears) in spring, to maintain the shape.

LAVANDULA

Prune back the previous year's growth to within 10cm (4in) of the ground in early or midspring if the plant is young. With larger, more established plants that have been pruned regularly, cut back to within 10cm (4in) of a framework of old wood.

With an old plant that has not been pruned routinely, just shorten the previous year's growth by about half in spring.

Above: Lavandula stoechas.

LAVATERA

L. arborea and *L. olbia* quickly grow tall, so prune annually in early or midspring. Cut the previous year's growth back to within about 15cm (6in) of the ground or the low framework of woody stumps. New growth may be slow at first, but it will put on a rapid spurt later.

LEYCESTERIA

Prune out the oldest third of the cane-like shoots each spring, cutting them off a couple of centimetres (1in) or so above the ground. This will ensure a constant supply of new stems without the top becoming too tall

or congested. Alternatively, you can use the lighter pruning method illustrated below.

1 The natural growth habit of leycesteria is upright. Horizontal and dead growth like this should be cut out, whichever method of pruning you use.

2 Minimal pruning also involves trimming back the ends of stems that are showing signs of die-back. Cut back to where there are replacement shoots.

3 With this method of pruning, the bush will still look well clothed at the top, but tidier. Try to avoid leaving long stubs, otherwise the hollow stems will die back and look unattractive.

LIGUSTRUM

Most ligustrums (the privets) are often seen as closely clipped hedging plants, but golden and variegated forms make attractive border shrubs.

You can give a specimen plant a clipped look simply by going over it with hand (hedge) shears once or twice a year, but they often look best in a border if allowed to grow naturally without any routine pruning.

If the shrub becomes too large, you can cut it back hard, to about 10cm (4in) above the ground if necessary, as it should make new growth.

LIPPIA, see Aloysia.

LONICERA, CLIMBING

The climbing species, the honeysuckles, are widely grown. They do not require routine pruning, but in time they are likely to become too large or too congested and tangled. Then they need attention.

The easiest to deal with are those that flower on the current year's growth, such as *L. japonica*, which you can prune drastically without a serious effect on the same year's flowers. You can simply clip them to size with hand (hedge) shears during the dormant season or in early spring.

The majority of species, including the highly popular *L. periclymenum*, flower on shoots that are at least a year old. If you prune these, the best time is as soon as flowering is over, and you must do it more selectively. If pruning is necessary, cut back the flowered shoot to a non-flowering shoot that will replace it.

See Pruning a Honeysuckle for how to cut back a neglected plant.

LONICERA, SHRUBBY

The various non-climbing loniceras have differing characteristics and pruning requirements.

L. nitida is best clipped to shape with hand (hedge) shears (see Shaping with Shears) in midspring, if you want a formal outline. For a more informal shape, no routine pruning is required, but you can use the technique of cutting out the oldest third of the stems (see The "One Third Method") if it becomes too large. The winter-flowering loniceras, such as *L. fragrantissima*, require no routine pruning.

MAHONIA

Most mahonias benefit from pruning. The popular species *M. aquifolium* and its varieties can make rampant growth. Prune established plants that have reached the desired size annually by cutting out the oldest third of the stems in early summer. You may also have to chop off stems which are spreading under-ground with a spade to limit the spread.

Prune ground-cover mahonias every second year by cutting them back to 15-30cm (6-12in) above the ground in spring. This will keep them compact with plenty of fresh new leaves.

Those species and varieties with stiff, upright growth, such as *M. lomariifolia* and *M. x media* 'Charity', will make bushier growth if you cut off the flower heads as soon as flowering is over. If there are no flowers at the tip of the tallest stems, remove the top rosette of leaves. This may only been needed for a couple of seasons, by which time the bushy habit will have been established.

Tall-growing mahonias would be bushier if you cut off dead flower heads back to a rosette of leaves. This is only necessary while the plants are young. Once the shrub has bushed out well it is not an annual task.

OLEARIA

Prune out the oldest one third of the shoots on mature plants in midsummer (see The "One Third Method") once flowering has finished.

OSMANTHUS

No routine pruning is required, but as these shrubs usually grow readily from old wood you can cut them back to size or shape if they become too large.

PAEONIA, SHRUBBY

No routine pruning is required, but cut out any dead wood in early summer. In cold regions winter damage is common, but it is best to wait until new growth is well established before deciding what needs to be cut out.

PARTHENOCISSUS

No routine pruning is required until these climbers outgrow their allotted space. Then it may be necessary to cut back far enough to keep the summer's growth away from windows and gutters, for example. (See Vines and Creepers.)

Above: Parthenocissus henryana *in autumn*.

PASSIFLORA

The species most likely to be grown outdoors is *P. caerulea*, and it is only likely to thrive as a vigorous climber in mild regions where winter frosts are not severe.

It will require pruning only once it outgrows its allotted space. In spring, decide which are your main framework branches, then cut back sideshoots from this to within one or two buds of their point of origin. This will restrict the amount of growth and prevent the plant becoming too tangled.

PAULOWNIA

When grown as a tree, this requires no routine pruning. It is sometimes grown as a shrub through hard annual pruning to encourage the production of extra-large leaves.

Cut the stems down to about 10cm (4in) above the ground each spring, before new growth starts to show. If you prune severely like this, the plant will respond to regular watering and feeding.

PERNETTYA, see Gaultheria.

PHILADELPHUS

Cut out the oldest third of the stems (see The "One Third Method") after flowering, usually in midsummer.

PHLOMIS

The shoots are often winter damaged in cold regions, but the plant will normally grow from old wood unless it is exceptionally old. To encourage the production of new shoots on compact plants, cut back the previous year's growth to about 10cm (4in) above the ground as soon as you see new growth in spring.

This is not essential, and you can just cut back sideshoots to within 5-10cm (2-4in) of the old framework of woody shoots instead.

PHORMIUM

No routine pruning is required, at most only the removal of any dead leaves may be necessary.

PHOTINIA (SYN. STRANVAESIA)

No routine pruning is required.

PIERIS

Above: Pieris formosa forrestii.

No routine pruning is required, but as this shrub will normally grow from old wood you can usually cut it back to size safely if it becomes too large.

PITTOSPORUM
No routine pruning is required, but a small specimen can be clipped to shape with hand (hedge) shears (see Shaping with Shears) if you want a compact shrub with a formal outline.

In cold regions winter damage and even death are not un-common. If affected, give the shrub a chance to show signs of life, then cut back to healthy wood. Sometimes shrubs will regrow if you cut them down almost to ground level – it may be worth a try if you think you have lost one.

POLYGONUM, see Fallopia.

POTENTILLA, SHRUBBY
Cut out the oldest third of the stems (see The "One Third Method") in early spring to keep the shrub compact and flower-ing well.

RHODODENDRON AND AZALEA
No routine pruning is required until the shrub begins to outgrow its space. Then you can start cutting out the oldest third of the stems annually to maintain a suitable shape and size. Dwarf kinds should not require any routine pruning.

To rejuvenate a very old and neglected plant, see Rejuvenating a Neglected Plant.

RHUS
No routine pruning is required. If suckering shoots appear (sometimes they come up in a nearby lawn) cut these back to their point of origin if possible.

RIBES
Cut out the oldest third of the stems (see The "One Third Method") immediately after flowering.

Above: Ribes sanguineum 'Brocklebankii'.

ROSMARINUS
Prune back sideshoots that grew last year to within 5-10cm (2-4in) of the woody framework of old branches, when flowering has finished.

RUBUS
Rubus cockburnianus, grown for its white winter stems, should be pruned back to ground level each spring (see Cutting to the Ground). Similar species can be treated in the same way.

For bushy species grown for their ornamental flowers, cut out the oldest third of the stems (see The "One Third Method") in midsummer.

RUSCUS
No routine pruning is required.

RUTA
Prune back the previous year's growth to within about 10cm (4in) of the ground if the plant has been pruned hard annually since it was young. If it already has a framework of old woody stems, cut back to within 5-10cm (2-4in) of these instead.

Be very careful when pruning, especially in sunshine. Contact can cause very severe allergic reactions. Wear gloves and do not let the sap or leaves get near your face, eyes, or bare arms.

Above: Ruta graveolens.

SALIX
Some salix are pruned regularly to stimulate the production of new stems, which are more colourful than old ones. These are widely planted for winter decoration. See Pruning for Colourful Stems for details of how to prune to create a shrubby effect. Salix are sometimes pruned to a short trunk (pollarded), by cutting the previous year's shoots back to within 2.5-5cm (1-2in) of the stump in early spring.

Other types of salix should not require routine annual pruning.

SALVIA
The shrubby salvia most often grown is S. officinalis, and its various varieties grown for their variegated foliage. In cold regions it often suffers winter damage and may even be killed. Routine pruning is required to improve the appearance after the winter, and to prevent the shrub becoming straggly.

If the plants have been pruned regularly and are not too woody, prune all the stems back to within about 10cm (4in) of the ground as soon as new growth can be seen in spring. Old plants that have not been pruned regularly and have an old woody frame-work of stems should be pruned by cutting back last year's shoots to within 5-10cm (2-4in) of these.

Above: Salvia officinalis 'Icterina'.

SAMBUCUS
Most sambucus will make more compact shrubs if you cut out the oldest third of the stems (see The "One Third Method") in midspring. Those grown for foliage effect, such as S. racemosa 'Plumosa Aurea', can be pruned very hard so that they remain relatively small but have much bigger leaves. Cut the shoots during the previous summer back to within about 5cm (2in) of the framework of old woody branches.

1 All the thin branches on this sambucus were produced the previous summer, so cutting them back close to the framework of old branches will ensure the shrub remains a similar size, with plenty of vigorous young growth.

2 Cut last summer's shoots back to within about 5cm (2in) of the old wood, taking it back to just above a pair of buds.

3 After pruning the plant will look rather mutilated, but as soon as the warm spring weather arrives the new shoots will grow rapidly.

SANTOLINA

If the plant has been hard pruned regularly, prune back the previous year's shoots to within 5-10cm (2-4in) of the ground (see Grey-leaved Foliage Plants) in midspring. If the plant is older and woodier, prune back to within about 2.5-5cm (1-2in) of the framework of old woody branches.

SARCOCOCCA

No routine pruning is required.

SKIMMIA

No routine pruning is required.

SENECIO, see Brachyglottis.

SORBARIA

Cut out the oldest third of the stems between late winter and midspring. A few species form a thicket of shoots that grow from ground level. To limit their spread, chop off with a spade, or saw off, while still young.

SPARTIUM

S. junceum is the only species and no routine pruning is required. An old bush can become tall and leggy, in which case prune back the previous year's growth to within 2.5-5cm (1-2in) of the old wood in spring when new growth starts.

SPIRAEA

It is important to decide which group your spiraea belongs to before pruning, as treatment varies. Most of them fall into one of the following two groups: **Spring-flowering** spiraeas, like *S. x arguta* and *S. x vanhouttei,* are best if the oldest third of the shoots are cut out (see The "One Third Method") after flowering, if the plant has reached its full size. **Summer-flowering** species, of

which *S. japonica* is a popular example, usually flower on shoots produced in the current year. Those that have growth resembling herbaceous plants can be cut down to within about 10cm (4in) of the ground in early or midspring. You may be able to use hand (hedge) shears. More woody types are best if the oldest third of the shoots are removed.

If you prefer, you can also simply shorten the tips of the plants in spring, just to restrain the shrub's size.

1 Twiggy summer-flowering spiraeas can be pruned in several ways. You may simply want to prune lightly to restrain spread.

2 In spring, shorten the shoots back to a point that allows for fresh summer growth.

3 The plant will look tidier after treatment, but it will still retain its basic shape and stature.

STRANVAESIA (SYN. PHOTINIA)

No routine pruning is required.

SYMPHORICARPOS

Cut out the oldest third of stems, in midsummer if this is practical. Some species form dense thickets which makes pruning difficult. If the bush seems out of hand, try cutting it down to about 5-10cm (2-4in) above the ground. It will probably regrow easily.

SYRINGA

S. vulgaris varieties are the ones most likely to benefit from routine pruning, as these become tall and often bare at the base with time. Each winter, saw or prune out about a quarter of the stems, choosing the oldest and the weakest.

Careful deadheading also helps. Cut the spent flower heads back to the first pair of leaves, as soon as possible after flowering has finished.

The bushier kinds, such as *S. microphylla,* often look good even without regular pruning. Once they become old and flower less well, however, it is worth cutting out the oldest third of the stems each spring.

TAMARIX

Routine pruning is not essential, but it will help to maintain a better shape. Check whether your particular shrub flowers on the current year's growth or on shoots produced the previous year. The first group, such as *T. ramosissima (syn. T. pentandra)*, should have last year's growth pruned back to within 5-8cm (2-3in) of the old wood.

Those that flower in spring on last year's shoots, such as *T. parviflora*, can have the previous year's growth shortened by about half after flowering.

Above: *Tamarix*.

ULEX

Routine pruning is not required, although you can trim it with hand (hedge) shears (see Shaping with Shears) if you want a neater, trimmed appearance. Do this in early summer, every second or third year if you want a less clipped appearance.

If the plant simply becomes too large, you might be able to rejuvenate it by cutting it back to about 15cm (6in) from the ground in early spring. New growth will usually appear from near the base.

VACCINIUM

No routine pruning is required.

VIBURNUM

There are many different kinds of viburnum, so make sure the specific advice applies to your particular shrub.

Winter- and spring-flowering species such as *V. tinus* and *V. carlesii* require no routine pruning. If a deciduous species such as *V. x bodnantense* becomes old and large, cut out one or two of the oldest stems each year until it looks attractive again. Do not do this annually. Cut out an old shoot only when those previously removed have been replaced by new shoots.

Those grown for foliage effect or fruits, such as *V. rhytidophyllum* and *V. opulus*, do not need pruning unless they become too large. Then you can remove one or two of the oldest stems in early summer, although this is not an annual job.

VINCA

These sprawling ground-cover plants will benefit from an annual trim to make the growth denser

Above: Vinca minor *'Aureo-marginata'*.

and perhaps encourage more flowers. Simply shear off the growth to several centimetres or inches above the ground in early spring. Use secateurs (pruning shears) or hand (hedge) shears. If you have a large area of vincas as ground cover you can even use a nylon line trimmer!

Above: Vinca major.

VITIS

Ornamental vines require routine pruning only when they have outgrown their allotted space, although those grown over a pergola will need cascading shoots snipped back regularly during the summer if they get in the way.

On established plants with a woody framework of branches, cut back the previous summer's growth to within one or two buds of the framework branches. This is best done during the dormant season.

If necessary, cut back over-vigorous summer growth to five or six leaves in midsummer (see also Vines and Creepers).

WEIGELA

Cut out the oldest third of the stems in midsummer.

YUCCA

No routine pruning is required.

Below: Weigela *'Majestueux'*.

Common Name Index

Azalea - *see* Rhododendron
Bay - *Laurus nobilis*
Beauty bush - *Kolkwitzia amabilis*
Bladder senna - *Colutea*
Bostin ivy - *Parthenocissus tricuspidata*
Broom - *Cytisus*, also *Genista*
Broom, Spanish - *Spartium junceum*
Butterfly bush - *Buddleja davidii*
Cabbage palm - *Cordyline*
Calico plant - *Kalmia latifolia*
Californian lilac - *Ceanothus*
Christmas box - *Sarcococca*
Climbing hydrangea - *Hydrangea petiolaris*
Contorted hazel - *Corylus avellana* 'Contorta'
Cotton lavender - *Santolina chamaecyprissus*
Curry plant - *Helichrysum angustifolium*
Dogwood - *Cornus alba, C. stolonifera*
Dutchman's pipe - *Aristolochia*
Elder - *Sambucus*
False castor oil plant - *Fatsia japonica*
Flowering currant - *Ribes sanguineum*
Golden privet - *Ligustrum ovalifolium* 'Aureum'
Gorse - *Ulex*
Hazel - *Corylus avellana*

Heather - *Calluna, Erica*
Holly - *Ilex*
Honeysuckle, shrubby - *Lonicera nitida*
Honeysuckle - *Lonicera periclymenum*
Ivy - *Hedera*
Japanese quince - *Chaenomeles*
Jasmine - *Jasminum*
Jew's mallow - *Kerria japonica*
Kolomikta vine - *Actinidia kolomikta*
Lavender - *Lavandula*
Lemon verbena - *Aloysia triphylla*
Lad's love - *Artemisia abrotanum*
Lilac - *Syringa*
Mexican orange blossom - *Choisya ternata*
Mock orange - *Philadelphus*
Passion flower - *Passiflora caerulea*
Peony - *Paeonia*
Perrywinkle - *Vinca*
Privet - *Ligustrum*
Privet, golden - *Ligustrum ovalifolium* 'Aureum'
Rock rose - *Cistus*, also *Helianthemum*
Rose of Sharon - *Hypericum calycinum*
Rosemary - *Rosmarinus*
Rue - *Ruta graveolens*

Russian vine - *Fallopia baldschuanica* (syn. *Polygonum baldschuanicum*)
Saint John's Wort - *Hypericum*
Sage - *Salvia officinalis*
Sea buckthorn - *Hippophae rhamnoides*
Silk tassel brush - *Garrya elliptica*
Smoke brush - *Cotinus coggygria*
Snowberry - *Symphoricarpos*
Southernwood - *Artemisia abrotanum*
Spanish broom - *Spartium junceum*
Sumach - *Rhus cotinus*
Sun rose - *Cistus*
Sweet bay - *Laurus nobilis*
Torbay palm - *Cardyline*
Tree peony - *Paeonia*
Virginia creeper - *Parthenocissus quinquefolia*
Vine, ornamental - *Vitis*
Whitewash bramble - *Rubus cockburnianus*
Willow - *Salix*
Winter jasmine - *Jasminum nudiflorum*
Wintersweet - *Chimonanthus*
Witch hazel - *Hamamelis*
Yew - *Taxus baccata*

INDEX

ACKNOWLEDGEMENTS

The Publishers would like to thank Capel Manor Horticultural and Environmental College, Bullsmoor Lane, Enfield EN1 4RQ, and Roger Sygrave in particular for all his help with the step-by-step photography. They would also like to thank Wilkinson Sword Group Ltd, 19 Brunel Way, London W3 (01656 655 595), Gardenia, 163 Parker Drive, Leicester LE4 OJP (0116 2340800), and The Fulham Palace Garden Centre, Bishops Avenue, London SW6 ((0171 736 2646) for their generosity in loaning equipment for the photography.

They would also like to thank the following people for allowing their pictures to be reproduced in this book: Peter McHoy for the pictures on pages 7, 11 (pruning knife), 14br, 17br, 19bl, 20b, 21br, 22br, 25b, 27b, 31bl, 31r, 34-1, 35br, 38tr, 42b, 43b, 52, 53, 54-2, 54-3, 55r, 57, 58-1, 58-2, 60b, 61b, 66-5, 69, 82, 83l, 85bl, 85br, 85tr, 86l, 86bl, 87, 89l, 89r, 90tr, 90br, 91l, 91m, 91r, 93, 94, 95 and 96.

The Garden Picture Library for the pictures on pages 76-1, 76-3, 76-4 (Photographer: Michael Howes); Photos Horticultural for the pictures on page 80; Harry Smith Collection for the pictures on pages 76-2 and 81.